Lake Superior

CANADA

MICHIGAN

Lake Huron

Lake Ontario

Lake Michigan

Lake Erie

Chicago

Lansing ★

INDIANA

Indianapolis ★

OHIO

Columbus ★

Cincinnati ●

VERMONT

Montpelier ★

NEW HAMPSHIRE

Concord ★

Boston ★

MASSACHUSETTS

Albany ★

Providence ★

NEW YORK

Hartford ★

RHODE ISLAND
CONNECTICUT

New York City ●

PENNSYLVANIA

NEW JERSEY

Trenton ★

Harrisburg ★

Philadelphia

Baltimore ●

Dover

DELAWARE

Washington, D.C. ★

Annapolis ★

MARYLAND

ATLANTIC OCEAN

St. Lawrence River

WEST VIRGINIA (1863)

Charleston ★

Richmond ★

Potomac R.

Chesapeake Bay

Frankfort ★

Ohio R.

Louisville ●

KENTUCKY

Hampton Roads ★

VIRGINIA

Fort Donelson

Nashville ★

Stones River (Murfreesboro) ✸

Fort Henry ✸

Tennessee R.

TENNESSEE

Shiloh ✸

Chattanooga ✸

Chickamauga ✸

Cumberland R.

Raleigh ★

NORTH CAROLINA

Columbia ★

SOUTH CAROLINA

Atlanta ★

ALABAMA

GEORGIA

Montgomery ★

Andersonville ■

Charleston ●

Fort Sumter ✸

Fort Wagner ✸

Port Royal ✸

Savannah

Mobile ●

Tallahassee ★

FLORIDA

Gulf of Mexico

0   100 miles

0   100 kilometers

Detail Map of Battles in Virginia, Maryland, and Pennsylvania

PENNSYLVANIA ✸ Gettysburg

MARYLAND

Antietam (Sharpsburg) ✸

WEST VIRGINIA

Harper's Ferry ✸

Potomac R.

Baltimore ●

N. Fork Shenandoah R.

S. Fork Shenandoah R.

Washington, D.C. ★

Manassas Junction (Bull Run) ✸

Chancellorsville ✸

Fredericksburg ✸

The Wilderness ✸

Rappahannock R.

Spotsylvania ✸

VIRGINIA

Cold Harbor ✸

Richmond ★

Seven Pines (Fair Oaks) ✸

Appomattox Courthouse ■

James R.

Petersburg ✸

Five Forks ✸

0   25 miles

0   25 kilometers

SCHOLASTIC ENCYCLOPEDIA OF THE CIVIL WAR

SCHOLASTIC ENCYCLOPEDIA OF THE CIVIL WAR

CATHERINE CLINTON

A FAIR STREET PRODUCTIONS BOOK

For Lizzy Rockwell
who has known me as a friend in need—
and has been an inspiration and a friend, indeed.

Library of Congress Cataloging-in-Publication
Clinton, Catherine 1952–
Scholastic Encyclopedia of the Civil War / by Catherine Clinton.
p. cm.
Includes index.
Summary: Traces the course of the Civil War, year by year, using profiles of important people,
    eyewitness accounts, and period art.
1.   United States—History—Civil War, 1861–1865—Encyclopedias, Juvenile.
[1. United States—History—Civil War, 1861–1865.]
I. Title
E468.C67   1999   98-45492
973.7' 03—dc21   CIP
                                         AC
ISBN: 0-590-37227-0

10 9 8 7 6 5 4 3 2 1   9/9 0/0 01 02 03
Printed in the U.S.A.   23
First printing, September 1999

Produced by Fairstreet Productions
Editor: Deborah Bull
Designer: Barbara Balch
Endpaper maps: David Lindroth, Inc.
Photo research coordinator: Shaie Dively, Photosearch Inc.
Consultants: Emory Thomas (University of Georgia) and Brian C. Pohanka

Cover photos: (top left, bottom right) The Granger Collection, NY;
(top right) Corbis-Bettmann; (bottom left) Collection of Herb Peck, Jr.

We thank Kate Waters at Scholastic for her enthusiastic support.

CONTENTS

CHAPTER I

Before the War

A NATION DIVIDING

T he United States wasn't even a nation when British surveyors Charles Mason and Jeremiah Dixon set out to draw the border between Pennsylvania and Maryland. This legendary boundary became known as the Mason-Dixon line. To the north lay free soil and to the south lay slavery. Mason and Dixon had only been charting a geographical divide, but North and South soon divided over much more than geography. No one single event, but a series of conflicts, pulled the country apart. And slavery, the system of holding black people in bondage, of treating humans as property, was at the heart of the divide. When the colonies first united to form a new nation, the states all tried to work together. But as America began to expand, tensions developed and fights broke out.

Compromises patched together by congressional leaders held the United States together for many years.

Over time, the free states of the North and the slave states of the South found it more and more difficult to resolve their differences. And when the South threatened to break away and form a separate country, America's very survival was at risk.

America was a land of North and South, urban and rural, industrial and agricultural, free and slave, during the decades leading up to the Civil War. These slaves in a Southern cotton field continued the African tradition of carrying baskets on their heads.

**BEFORE THE WAR
AT-A-GLANCE**

1820
Missouri Compromise

1831
Antislavery Newspaper
The Liberator

1850
The Compromise of 1850

1854
Kansas-Nebraska Act

1857
Dred Scott Decision

1859
John Brown's Raid
Harpers Ferry, Virginia

1860
November: Abraham Lincoln
elected president

December: South Carolina
secedes from the Union

A busy street in New York City during the 1850s.

In 1820 any visitor to the largest city in the North and the biggest city in the South could see important differences between these two major sections, or regions, within America. The differences led to "sectional conflict," friction between the sections or competing regions. In New York City, the largest city in America (population 124,000), not only were the docks stocked with goods from all over the world, but they also bustled with ships full of European immigrants seeking a fresh start in a promising young country. Northern city streets were lined with banks and shops, soon to be linked by rail lines, and dotted with factories. Northerners, known as Yankees, took pride in their expanding commerce.

By contrast, in New Orleans, Louisiana, the fifth-largest city in America and the only sizable one in the South (population 27,000), the docks were crowded with sugar, cotton, and slaves. These were symbols of the plantations, large farms in the South where planters used slaves to work the land. The South was an expanding region as well, but plantation agriculture led the economy. Although slaveholding households were not in the majority, the region became known as the "Slave South" because slave owners controlled the state legislatures and governors' mansions there.

The expansion of the plantation economy pulled the South in a different direction than the North. White Southerners celebrated a different way of life, a society that exploited slave labor and considered even free African Americans as second-class citizens. Though

EYEWITNESS

"We have here before us a cotton plantation with slaves picking cotton. The usual task for a man is eighty pounds per day; for a woman, seventy pounds; but they often work them far above this task. During the task time, if a slave fails to accomplish this task, he receives five cuts with the cat-o'-nine-tails, or the negro whip, for every pound of cotton that is wanting to make up the requisite number. In the distance you will observe a woman being whipped at the whipping post, near which are the scales for weighing the cotton."

WILLIAM WELLS BROWN,
Panorama of Slavery

The Missouri Compromise

By 1819, when the territory of Missouri applied for admission to the Union as our twenty-third state, congressional leaders were in an uproar. A Southern congressman shook his fist while addressing the House of Representatives and challenged, "You have kindled a fire which a sea of blood can only extinguish." A Northern congressman bellowed back, "If civil war must come, let it come." Former president Thomas Jefferson, though a slaveholder, shuddered at the angry debate, comparing it to "a fire bell in the night" that warned of impending disaster.

Former president James Madison saw the quarrel as a kind of family brawl. Madison suggested that the North and South were like a husband and wife whose children displayed the traits of one of their parents. When too many children resembled their mother, the slave states, their stern father objected. The "stain of slavery," Madison argued, had marked the family from the beginning, and it could not easily be removed. In this heated debate over the nation's future, the family metaphor arose again and again.

When territories—regions annexed by the government but not yet organized into states—applied to join the Union, congressional leaders tried to preserve the balance between free and slave states. The South especially needed a balance to retain its influence in the Senate, where each state had two senators; but the North, whose population was exploding, increasingly controlled the House of Representatives, where the size of a state's delegation was determined by its population.

Before the Louisiana Purchase in 1803, both the Mason-Dixon line and the Ohio River formed a boundary between Northern and Southern states. When territories west of the Mississippi River began to apply to become states, conflicts erupted. Statesman Henry Clay of Kentucky helped to work out a legislative package known as the Missouri Compromise: Missouri would be admitted as a slave state, and Maine would separate from Massachusetts and form a free state. In addition, any future states applying for admission from the Louisiana Territory would be free if they were north of Missouri's southern boundary, and slave if they were south of it. Both proslavery advocates and antislavery radicals were displeased by this agreement, but everyone thought the matter was finally settled.

blacks were also second-class citizens in the North, slavery there was on the decline, outlawed state by state after the Revolution.

Southern leaders in Congress resented the North's promotion of manufacturing and transportation. The North was always urging the federal government to fund projects like interstate roads and canals. The South was angered by the North's support of tariffs, which are taxes on imported goods. After all, colonists had once dumped tea into Boston Harbor to protest tariffs, an event that propelled the British colonists along the road to the American Revolution! Now, the South did not want to pay taxes they felt were unfair, and they complained loudly.

In the North, politicians opposed the extension of slavery into the West, where small farmers wanted to work their own land and not compete with the large plantations run by slave labor, which slave owners championed. The two conflicting groups clashed in the western territories.

HENRY CLAY

In 1828 Congress passed a high tariff to help Northern manufacturers compete with imported foreign goods. The South roared its disapproval, labeling the law the Tariff of Abominations. Southern statesman John C. Calhoun of South Carolina called the tariff unconstitutional and wrote a document entitled the "South Carolina Exposition and Protest," which for the first time clearly spelled out the South's political opposition to the interference of the federal government in the affairs of individual states. Some statesmen felt that the federal government was overextending its powers, and Calhoun argued that any state could refuse to enforce laws which were not legal according to the U.S. Constitution. This argument was called the doctrine of nullification. Calhoun argued that a state could "nullify," or refuse to obey, any unconstitutional law imposed by the federal government. This doctrine seemed to favor the rights of states over the right of the federal government to speak for all states.

JOHN C. CALHOUN

Calhoun's position was so rigid that he was finally forced to choose between the United States and his home state of South Carolina. Eventually he sided with South Carolina against the federal government, showing that he was totally committed to the doctrine of states' rights.

Sectional disputes and states' rights debates mushroomed, and by 1830 the doctrine of nullification was bitterly contested in Congress. Some Northern politicians wanted Southern statesmen to come to their senses and recognize

In the 1830s, visitors and residents often enjoyed a leisurely stroll along the East Battery in Charleston, South Carolina. Boats filled the harbor in this port city on the Atlantic.

By the 1840s more slaves lived in New Orleans than in any other city in the United States. This Louisiana port shipped thousands of bales of cotton to Europe, when cotton accounted for 60 percent of America's exports.

that unity and compromise were essential to keeping the country strong. Massachusetts statesman Daniel Webster gave a moving speech that defended the federal government, and he concluded by stating, "Liberty and Union, now and forever, one and inseparable."

But increasingly, the political and economic interests of North and South diverged. Even though the federal government lowered the existing tariff in 1832, Southern politicians continued to dissent. Their protest movement was headed by the champion of nullification, John C. Calhoun. During the winter of 1832–33, tensions that threatened to escalate into more than just a war of words erupted between South Carolina and the federal government. A political standoff occurred when South Carolina threatened to defy federal law, refuse to obey the tariff, and stop collecting taxes for the federal government on imports into South Carolina.

President Andrew Jackson threatened to use force to make South Carolina obey, declaring: "If one drop of blood be shed there in defiance of the laws of the United States, I will hang the first man of them I can get my hands on to the first tree I can find." These were fighting words, but conflict was avoided when, once again, a compromise was worked out by Senator Henry Clay, who truly earned his nickname, the "Great Compromiser." The truce was only temporary, however, because Calhoun was prepared to resign his position as vice president rather than support policy that conflicted with his faith in states' rights. Calhoun's loyalty to his beliefs demonstrated that political alliances might not hold when men were more interested in protecting the rights of their states than in advancing a national political agenda.

War with Mexico (1846–48)

U.S. troops landing in Mexico at Vera Cruz.

After Texas broke off from Spain to establish an independent republic in 1836, Texans asked to be annexed to the United States. When Texas applied to the federal government to become a territory in 1845, congressional leaders divided over the issue. Southerners welcomed Texas into the United States because of its rich new lands where slavery could expand. But Northerners feared that Texas could become not one, but many, slave states. Even a single large additional state would upset the delicate sectional balance.

In 1845, however, Texas did become a U.S. territory, and the following year, President James K. Polk sent troops along the border separating Texas and Mexico. When fighting broke out, the United States declared war. Soon the U.S. troops, under Generals Zachary Taylor and Winfield Scott, won great victories. The capture of the capital, Mexico City, in 1847 secured the defeat of Mexico. Although it gave the United States a vast new territory, the peace treaty triggered a new round of debates over the question of slavery.

WILLIAM LLOYD GARRISON

"We must instantly burst the shackles of slaves. IMMEDIATE EMANCIPATION alone can save the South and the nation from the vengeance of Heaven!" With these words Boston editor William Lloyd Garrison launched his abolitionist newspaper, *The Liberator,* in 1831. Garrison was at the forefront of a movement to "abolish" (do away with) slavery and "emancipate" (free) slaves immediately, not by any gradual means. His followers were called abolitionists. Some of these abolitionists were Quakers, members of a Protestant sect known as the Society of Friends. The abolitionists formed local, state, and even national antislavery societies. The United States had banned the importation of slaves in 1807, all Northern states had passed laws against slavery by the 1830s, and now abolitionists wanted to outlaw slavery everywhere.

Under the harsh slavery laws, slaves often were denied the right to marry, to raise their own children, and to use their own labor to support their families. Instead, white owners were given total control over their human "property." Slaves could be punished with whips and chains. The cruelty of the auction block, where husbands were sold without their wives and children were separated from their parents, caused a growing number of Americans in both the North and the South to oppose the South's "peculiar institution," as slavery was known.

In the South, slave owners were outraged by the abolitionists' attacks upon their way of life. At the same time, a slave preacher in Southampton, Virginia, named Nat Turner urged his fellow slaves to rise up and kill their masters. Now slaves were taking action. In August 1831, when more than fifty whites died in a rebellion led by Turner, Southerners blamed abolitionists for the bloodshed. Southern politicians believed the antislavery movement had to be stopped. The war over slavery was heating up.

Frederick Douglass

The most important African-American leader of the nineteenth century was born a slave on the eastern shore of Maryland in 1817. At the age of twenty-one, he escaped slavery. Douglass created one of the first abolitionist newspapers, *The North Star,* in his adopted home of Rochester, New York. In 1845 he published his remarkable *Narrative of the Life of Frederick Douglass, an American Slave,* which recounted the harshness of slavery, his years as a fugitive, his triumph over hardship, and his commitment to seeking freedom and equality for all Americans, including his fellow African Americans. Douglass was a powerful voice for abolitionism. In an Independence Day speech in 1852, he proclaimed to his mostly white audience: "The Fourth of July is yours, not mine. You may rejoice, I must mourn."

LEFT: Abolitionists attend a rally in Cazenovia, New York. Frederick Douglass (at the left of the table) was among the speakers.

The Underground Railroad

During the years preceding the Civil War, travelers in the South might have seen a sign nailed to a tree that read, "Runaway slave, prime condition, 18 years or thereabouts. Answers to the name of Toby. Property of Jeremiah Higgens." Slave owners hired bounty hunters with bloodhounds and rifles to chase down runaways.

But many runaway slaves, maybe even Toby, escaped to freedom on the Underground Railroad. This was not really a railroad, nor was it underground. It was a network of people who transported fugitive slaves into one of the fourteen free states in the North or into Canada. The network was called the Underground Railroad because most of the smuggling activities took place in darkness and in secret. More than three thousand people opposed to slavery participated. Slaves were known as "freight" and were assisted in their escapes by people called "conductors." The safe houses and resting places, usually located a night's walk apart, were referred to as "stations," and routes to freedom were called "lines."

Runaways often wore elaborate disguises, including wigs and mustaches. Ellen Craft, a light-skinned slave who escaped to freedom, pretended to be a white man accompanied by a slave, William, who was really her husband. One of the most famous conductors on the Underground Railroad was a former slave named Harriet Tubman, who became known as the Moses of her people.

Of course, not all those who tried to escape on the Underground Railroad made their way to safety. Many slaves were captured and sent back to their masters for a whipping or worse. A large number of slaves did escape, but because secrecy was essential, exact numbers are not known. The activities of the Underground Railroad helped convince the white South that the abolitionists in the North would never abandon their commitment to antislavery. The North's fight against slavery was an important factor that contributed to the outbreak of the Civil War.

Harriet Tubman (standing at left) poses with a slave family she helped to liberate on the Underground Railroad.

Henry Clay, earning his nickname the "Great Compromiser," outlines the Compromise of 1850 to his fellow congressmen.

By the terms of the peace treaty with Mexico, the United States gained a large chunk of new territory, a region that comprises present-day California, Nevada, Utah, and Arizona as well as parts of New Mexico, Colorado, and Wyoming. Once again, Congress debated what would be done with these new lands. Should they be slave or free? Henry Clay of Kentucky joined Daniel Webster of Massachusetts and Stephen Douglas of Illinois to work out a solution. In 1850 Congress decided to admit California into the Union as a free state and to abolish the slave trade in the District of Columbia. Congress also created two neutral territories in Utah and New Mexico that were not designated to either side of the issue, but were "with or without slavery, as its constitution may prescribe." In addition, the legislature passed a new Fugitive Slave Act, whereby the federal government pledged to assist owners searching for

EYEWITNESS

"*What is life to me if I am to be a slave in Tennessee? My neighbors! I have lived with you many years, and you know me. My home is here, and my children were born here. I am bound to Syracuse by pecuniary [financial] interests, and social and family bonds. And do you think I can be taken away from you and from my wife and children and be a slave in Tennessee? . . . Some kind and good friends advise me to quit my country and stay in Canada until this tempest is passed. . . . But my conviction is strong. . . . I tell you, the people of Syracuse and of the whole North must meet this tyranny and crush it by force, or be crushed by it. . . . The time has come to change the tones of submission into tones of defiance,—and to tell Mr. Fillmore [the president, Millard Fillmore] . . . to send on their bloodhounds. . . .*"

REV. J. W. LOGUEN,
an escaped slave, speaking
against the Fugitive Slave Act
in Syracuse, New York,
October 4, 1850

Most main streets of any sizable Southern town featured at least one slave trader, where auctions might be held.

$150 REWARD.

RAN AWAY FROM THE SUBSCRIBER, ON THE NIGHT OF THE 27TH OCTOBER,

A Negro Man named Ben,

Calling himself BEN. THOMAS.—On the day he absconded, by means of false keys, he opened a desk and took therefrom about two hundred Dollars in specie, 20 Dollars of which was in gold half Eagles, and nearly the whole of the balance in American half Dollars. In addition to

Ads for runaways, such as the one above, ran in most Southern newspapers before the war. Owners hoped to apprehend fugitive slaves by providing descriptions and promising rewards.

runaway slaves. Congressional leaders hammered out these terms in a final settlement that became known as the Compromise of 1850. Congress hotly debated the issues of sectional conflict, and many important people sat in the gallery to hear the greatest political debates of the day. After many months of speeches, Senator Stephen Douglas proclaimed with relief, "I have determined never to make another speech on the slavery question." He would soon be proved very wrong.

FIGHTING THE SLAVE CATCHERS

Blacks in the North felt endangered by ruthless bounty hunters, known as slave catchers, who roamed the countryside looking for fugitives. Sometimes these slave catchers even kidnapped slaves and sold them illegally. Antislavery supporters resisted bravely, especially at a small town in southeastern Pennsylvania called Christiana. In September 1851, a Maryland slave owner and his band of slave catchers, armed with shotguns and federal warrants, surrounded the house of William Parker, a local black leader, and demanded the surrender of four slaves hidden inside. When Parker refused, gunfire erupted and Parker killed one man and wounded three others.

When news of this "riot" reached nearby Washington, President Millard Fillmore sent the marines; but by the time these federal troops arrived, the blacks involved had fled. Thirty-six blacks and two whites were arrested. This incident symbolized abolitionists' growing resistance to the rights of slaveholders.

Another case exploded in the headlines when Anthony Burns, a runaway slave, was captured in Boston in May 1854. A mob stormed the courthouse where Burns was held and tried to free him, but the rescue attempt failed. Nearly fifty thousand people gathered to witness the procession as Burns was marched down the courthouse steps and along streets to the docks to be sent back to slavery. All along the route, buildings were draped in black. The dejected Burns was transported back to his master in Virginia.

A Story of Slavery

When she was very young, Harriet Beecher wrote stories, and when she grew up, she became a writer whose work influenced millions. She was one of several children born to New England minister Lyman Beecher, a famous religious leader and a strong antislavery advocate. Harriet was very close to her older sister Catharine, who became a writer, too.

When Harriet's father became head of a seminary in 1832, the Beecher family moved to Cincinnati where he continued his abolitionist activities. In Cincinnati, Harriet met and, in 1836, married Calvin Stowe.

When antislavery debates flared over the Compromise of 1850, Harriet Beecher Stowe began to write a story about slavery. In 1852 she published her novel, *Uncle Tom's Cabin,* feeling that "I had written some of it almost with my heart's blood."

The book sold more than three hundred thousand copies in America in one year and more than a million and a half in England. The author drew on her knowledge of the Underground Railroad to tell the story of a runaway slave, Eliza, who crosses a frozen river with her baby in her arms in her bid for freedom. The tale of the devoted Kentucky slave, Uncle Tom, and the angelic daughter of his owner, Little Eva, touched millions of readers and converted thousands of people to the antislavery cause.

When the Compromise of 1850 offered Utah and New Mexico a chance to vote on whether to become a free or slave state, many people protested. The compromise seemed to give the new territories an unfair advantage, and the older territories that were part of the Louisiana Purchase complained that they wanted a choice, too. They demanded an equal right to vote on the slave question and not be subjected to the terms of the Missouri Compromise, which established a geographical divide between the Northern (free) and Southern (slave) states.

Stephen Douglas, the senator from Illinois, believed that Kansas and Nebraska should be given the same rights and began making speeches again. He proposed allowing each state to decide its own destiny when it applied to enter the Union. When Congress passed the Kansas-Nebraska Act in 1854, the law effectively repealed, or did away with, the Missouri Compromise of 1820, which had drawn a line across the nation. States north of this line had been free; states south of the line had been slave.

DID YOU KNOW?

Abolitionist settlers who moved to Kansas carried rifles that were nicknamed "Beecher's Bibles" after the antislavery spokesman Reverend Henry Ward Beecher. He was Harriet Beecher Stowe's brother.

1857

Dred Scott Decision

"Am I not a man, and a brother?" became the slogan of the American Antislavery Society. By the 1850s abolitionists wanted the slavery question to be decided on a more human and personal level. In an important legal case, *Dred Scott* v. *Sandford,* the slavery question went all the way to the U.S. Supreme Court. Americans hoped that the highest court in the land could resolve this agonizing conflict.

Dred Scott, the slave of an army doctor in Missouri, a slave state, accompanied his master when he moved to a free state. Scott sued for his freedom, and the case dragged on for more than a decade. In 1857 the Supreme Court justices handed down their landmark ruling, known as the Dred Scott decision.

DRED SCOTT

The Supreme Court ruled against Dred Scott. The justices decided that the Missouri Compromise had been *unconstitutional* because it denied slave owners their property rights. Their decision also opened all the western lands to slaveholders. Further, the Supreme Court declared that African Americans could not sue in federal court for their freedom, as Dred Scott had done, because they were not legally citizens of the United States. This ruling was a terrible disappointment to the abolitionist community and was a shattering blow to both slaves and to free blacks. Many white reformers as well felt that the Court's ruling had put the "nail in the coffin" of equality for African Americans.

The Free-Soil Battery guard in Kansas stands ready to use weapons against invading proslavery forces. Before the Kansas border war began in 1856, this cannon was probably only used to fire salutes at Fourth of July celebrations.

Proslavery politicians rejoiced. By the 1850s cotton was the number one U.S. export, and the South would do anything to maintain its booming plantation economy. South Carolina Senator James Henry Hammond jubilantly declared, "Cotton is king!" Opponents of the Kansas-Nebraska Act mounted protest campaigns, and in 1854 they formed their own political party—the Republican party. Some members of the Free-Soil party, which had been established in 1848, joined with the Republicans, bringing along their slogan, "Free soil, free labor, free speech and free men."

This free-for-all atmosphere turned Kansas into a battleground because both sides repeatedly resorted to violence. "Border ruffians," as the armed supporters of slavery were known, cast illegal votes and threatened violence against opponents who tried to vote. In May 1856 seven hundred outlaw soldiers, known as guerrillas, sacked and burned the antislavery settlement of Lawrence, Kansas. Local abolitionists fought back with equal violence, and this conflict in Kansas became known as the "border war."

In one notorious example, John Brown, a recent migrant to Kansas from the East and a passionate advocate of abolitionism, led a group of seven, including his sons, on a midnight raid of a proslavery settlement along the Pottawatomie River. Brown and his sons dragged men from their beds and killed them in cold blood. Politicians in the North and South, hearing about this violence and revenge, feared that the lawlessness in "Bleeding Kansas" would soon spread throughout the country.

The Caning of Senator Sumner

"THWACK, THWACK!" On May 22, 1856, a stunned crowd watched South Carolina Congressman Preston Brooks land blow after blow on Senator Charles Sumner of Massachusetts. Only two days before, Sumner had given a stirring speech against slavery in which he criticized a fellow senator, who happened to be Brooks's uncle. To defend his uncle's honor, Brooks used his walking stick on Sumner, "caning" him into submission.

Never before had such a display of violence erupted in the Capitol chambers. Onlookers were horrified as the middle-aged, though vigorous, Sumner was helplessly pinned to his seat. Even after Sumner stumbled and collapsed onto the floor, Brooks kept beating him with his broken cane.

Following a public outcry, Brooks resigned from the House of Representatives, but was reelected by an overwhelming majority. Though he recuperated from this brutal beating, Sumner was unable to return to the Senate for more than three years. His empty chair in the Senate chamber was a reminder of the violence that was provoked by the debates over slavery.

LEFT: Harpers Ferry was just a quiet village of 2,000 on the banks of the Shenandoah River when John Brown launched his famous raid in 1859.

A young John Brown takes the Pledge of Allegiance.

JOHN BROWN'S RAID
HARPERS FERRY, VIRGINIA, OCTOBER 1859

The sleepy depot at Harpers Ferry was an unlikely place for John Brown to begin his private war on slavery. After returning east from Kansas, he was all fired up about raising an army of freedom fighters to invade the South and emancipate, or free, slaves by force. He talked to other abolitionists, including Frederick Douglass, William Lloyd Garrison, and Harriet Tubman. Although many found Brown's fanatic politics and violent plots alarming, few expected him to act.

On the morning of October 16, Brown and eighteen of his followers (thirteen whites and five blacks) cut the telegraph lines and seized the federal arsenal, a military weapons warehouse, at Harpers Ferry, Virginia. The raiders hoped to take guns, pass them out to slaves, and move through the countryside gathering rebels. Brown and his men didn't get far. The abolitionist band took hostages inside the arsenal as federal troops descended on them. Colonel Robert E. Lee, the federal officer in charge, was finally able to recapture the arsenal, where he found several of Brown's men dead inside and Brown himself wounded.

John Brown and his followers were put on trial. Brown was found guilty of treason and murder, sentenced to death, and hanged on December 2, 1859, in Virginia. One of his black comrades, John Copeland, wrote before he, too, was executed, "I am not terrified by the gallows which I see staring me in the face, and upon which I am soon to stand and suffer death for doing what George Washington was made a hero for doing. . . . Washington entered the field to fight for the freedom of the American people—not for the white man alone, but for both black and white."

Despite his violence John Brown became a hero to many abolitionists in the North, but was despised in the South. Divided responses to Brown's attack on

Cassius Clay
THE ANTISLAVERY SOUTHERNER

Only a few maverick leaders in the South opposed slavery. Born in 1810 into a slave-owning family in Kentucky, Cassius Clay supported racial equality and pursued a lifelong crusade against slavery. In 1845 he began to publish an antislavery newspaper called *The True American*. Clay took a daring stand by establishing an integrated community of blacks and whites who worked together at Berea, Kentucky. Proslavery violence forced the group to disband, but Clay would not back down. He became a strong supporter of Abraham Lincoln, who as president rewarded Clay by offering him a diplomatic post in Russia.

Harpers Ferry sharpened the contrast between North and South and deepened the divide between these two sections of the country.

THE ELECTION OF 1860
NOVEMBER 6

During the summer of 1860, the Republicans nominated Abraham Lincoln for president, in spite of his relative inexperience. "Honest Abe," as he was known, had served only one term as an Illinois delegate in the House of Representatives and just four terms in the Illinois state legislature. But Lincoln had proved himself a worthy contestant in his Senate race against Stephen Douglas, when the Lincoln-Douglas debates launched his national fame. Also nicknamed "the Railsplitter" because he spent much of his impoverished youth chopping wood, Lincoln became a symbol of Republican party values.

The election of 1860 was a heated contest for the White House because four major candidates had entered the race. This large number of nominees split the presidential vote considerably. Lincoln won only 39 percent of the popular vote, but the *majority* of electoral votes, allowing him to claim the presidency.

Southern responses to Lincoln's victory reflected horror. Disgruntled voters in Louisiana had supposedly put a price on the president-elect's head and were willing to pay $40,000 to any successful assassin. Lincoln considered this wild talk all bluff. The country had faced many moments of conflict and crisis before, and differences always seemed to get resolved.

SOUTH CAROLINA ORDINANCE OF SECESSION
DECEMBER 20, 1860

"Hang him! String Abe up!" "Death to tyrants!" "This means war!" These were the angry words shouted by "fire-eaters," the nickname given to Southerners who wanted to secede from the Union. A protest convention held in Charleston in December produced the Ordinance of Secession, which declared South Carolina's intent to secede, to be the first state to quit the Union and form an independent nation, the Confederate States of America.

Lincoln and his supporters hoped this crisis, like other controversies, would soon blow over. At the close of 1860, weary politicians did not know how long a compromise might take, and many feared the consequences if no middle ground could be found. As families gathered together over the Christmas holidays, all felt themselves at the crossroads, unsure of what the new year might bring.

Lincoln addressing the crowd. Douglas is seated at the left of the painting.

CHAPTER 2

1861

The year opened under clouds of uncertainty. Although the North and South had fought over their differences before, Americans feared that no compromise could be reached this time. And what would happen if more Southern states followed South Carolina's lead and left the Union? What should newly elected Abraham Lincoln do?

Early in the new year, all eyes turned to Charleston, South Carolina, where the federal government's troops were trapped on an island fort in Charleston's harbor and running out of supplies. Tensions ran high, and early one April morning the Confederates opened fire. The Union commander was forced to surrender Fort Sumter. Following this military encounter, Lincoln issued a call for volunteer soldiers, and Americans had to face their fears: The war had finally come.

From the rocky shores of Maine to the plains of Texas, thousands marched off to enlist and perhaps give their lives for their country. Generals and their armies prepared for combat. In July, Confederate and Union soldiers met in their first great wartime encounter at Bull Run, near Manassas Junction, Virginia.

What began as an old quarrel over slavery and states' rights grew into an enormous new battle, a fight to the death, some feared. This struggle would decide not only the future of the country, but as the United States expanded west, the destiny of the entire continent.

"WAR!" This cry rallied thousands of volunteers, including the soldiers from New York's Seventh Regiment in the painting at the left.

THE YEAR AT-A-GLANCE

January
Five Southern states join South Carolina and secede

February 18
Jefferson Davis sworn in as first Confederate president

March 4
Abraham Lincoln sworn in as sixteenth U.S. president

April 12–14
Battle of Fort Sumter
Charleston, South Carolina

July 21
First Battle of Bull Run
Manassas Junction, Virginia

November 1
George McClellan appointed General in Chief of Union army

November 7
Union gunboats capture Port Royal, South Carolina

JEFFERSON DAVIS

West Point graduate Jefferson Davis had been a hero of the Mexican War and U.S. Secretary of War under President Franklin Pierce. When the Southern states began to leave the Union, Davis decided to give up his Senate seat from his home state, Mississippi. He was cutting flowers in the rose garden on his plantation, when a telegram arrived on February 10 to inform him that he had been chosen to be the first president of the Confederacy! He was to go at once to the new Confederate capital, Montgomery, Alabama, for his inauguration. His vice president, Alexander Stephens, was a former congressman from Georgia.

Davis headed for Alabama with a heavy heart. On February 18, he took the oath of office on the steps of the Alabama capitol building. When he kissed the Bible at the ceremony's conclusion, the crowd gave their new leader a rousing cheer. Davis pledged to uphold states' rights and not to interfere with slave owners.

The entire country trembled with anticipation at what might happen next! Some Confederates claimed they would fight for independence, just as the patriots of the American Revolution had fought in 1776. But how could there be two presidents? two governments?

Some secessionists hoped they could gain their independence without war. Senator James Chesnut of South Carolina knew his fellow Rebels were itching to "whip the Yankees," but he hoped to avoid war. Chesnut boasted that he was

CONFEDERATE STATES

STATE	SECEDED	READMITTED
SOUTH CAROLINA	Dec. 20, 1860	July 9, 1868
MISSISSIPPI	Jan. 9, 1861	Feb. 23, 1870
FLORIDA	Jan. 10, 1861	June 25, 1868
ALABAMA	Jan. 11, 1861	July 13, 1868
GEORGIA	Jan. 19, 1861	July 15, 1870
LOUISIANA	Jan. 26, 1861	July 9, 1868
TEXAS	Feb. 1, 1861	March 30, 1870
VIRGINIA	April 17, 1861	Jan. 26, 1870
ARKANSAS	May 6, 1861	June 22, 1868
TENNESSEE	May 7, 1861	July 24, 1866
NORTH CAROLINA	May 20, 1861	July 4, 1868

Border States

When South Carolina rebelled against the federal government, many other states were undecided about what to do: Should they stay with the Union or join their Southern brothers in a bid for independence? In this difficult situation, North Carolina had the hardest time deciding and hesitated even after Virginia to the north and South Carolina to the south had already joined the new Southern nation, the Confederacy.

Lincoln worried about the states on the border between North and South—Maryland, Delaware, Kentucky, and Missouri. In those states slavery was still legal, and Lincoln promised not to interfere with slave owners if these states would remain

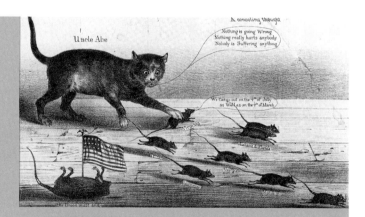

Abe Lincoln is the "cat" trying to keep the "mice" (slave states) from running away—fleeing the Union—in this 1861 cartoon.

loyal to the Union. Lincoln's strategy worked, and in 1862 the western part of Virginia seceded from the state, returning to the Union as the new state of West Virginia in 1863.

willing to drink all the blood shed as a consequence of secession because he was so sure that there wouldn't be any! In the early months of 1861, white Southerners claimed that a thimbleful of blood was worth Confederate independence.

But Confederate Vice President Alexander Stephens, a good friend of Lincoln's while the two were in Congress, was worried. He felt that "revolutions are much easier started than controlled."

On February 11, the day Jefferson Davis departed from his Mississippi home, Abraham Lincoln left his hometown in Illinois for his inauguration in Washington, D.C. When the lanky former congressman boarded a train in Springfield, Illinois, he embarked on a much longer and more dangerous journey than he realized. Having spent most of his life among friends on the western frontier, Lincoln now had to go to Washington to try to prevent the country from tearing itself apart over slavery and states' rights.

The president-elect wanted to persuade North and South to stay together, but first he had to arrive safely in Washington and take office. When death threats and pro-Confederate riots in Maryland made the trip dangerous, Lincoln was forced to wear a disguise and make his way from Baltimore to Washington under the cover of night.

On Inauguration Day, however, Lincoln stood tall in his stovepipe hat. More than thirty thousand people gathered on a chilly March morning to hear the sixteenth president of the United States take office. Lincoln promised to leave slavery alone where it already existed and reminded Americans of the "bonds of affection" between North and South. Even as he hoped "the better angels of our nature" would keep the country from going to war, he threatened to use force if necessary to hold the Union together.

Lincoln's First Inaugural was held in the shadow of the Capitol building—still under construction.

DID YOU KNOW?

Abraham Lincoln and Jefferson Davis were both born in Kentucky, less than one hundred miles apart and within nine months of each other.

Prior to becoming President, Lincoln was beardless.

W hen South Carolina declared its independence on December 20, Major Robert Anderson, a federal officer stationed just outside Charleston, knew there might be trouble. On the day after Christmas in 1860, he moved his troops onto the man-made island in Charleston's harbor known as Fort Sumter.

Lincoln wanted to send Anderson supplies, but the Confederates insisted they would fire on any federal ships that "invaded." After months of negotiations with the government of South Carolina failed, President Lincoln announced he was sending food and supplies to Fort Sumter. On April 11 newly commissioned Confederate General P.G.T. Beauregard issued the federal commander at the fort, Major Anderson, an ultimatum: Evacuate the island, or the Confederates would open fire on the fort. To Beauregard's astonishment, Anderson and his men refused to desert their post.

Before dawn the next morning, the Confederates began their bombardment, awakening Charleston's residents with a deafening display of firepower. Over the next day and a half, Southern troops fired more than thirty-five hundred artillery shells while citizens watched and cheered. After withstanding nearly six hundred direct hits, which left the fort battered and crumbling, the Union commander surrendered at 2:30 P.M. on April 13.

DID YOU KNOW?

Robert Anderson, the Union commander in charge of Fort Sumter, was completely loyal to the Union. That allegiance was hard for him because he was a Kentuckian and his wife was the daughter of the governor of Georgia, a staunch supporter of the Confederacy. Anderson's family was one of thousands across America whose loyalties were divided. The Civil War became known as the "brothers' war," but it was often the "brothers-in-law's war."

Women and children watch from Charleston's rooftops as the shells rain down on Fort Sumter on April 12. When this image of the bombardment appeared in *Harper's Weekly*, the war came alive for thousands of readers.

NORTH

MARY LIVERMORE, Boston, Massachusetts
"As they [Union soldiers] marched from the railroad stations, they were escorted by crowds cheering vociferously. Merchants and clerks rushed out from stores, bareheaded, saluting them as they passed. Windows were flung up; and women leaned out into the rain, waving flags and handkerchiefs. . . . I had never seen anything like this before."

SOUTH

RALPH SEMMES, New Orleans, Louisiana
"War now occupied the thoughts of the multitude, and the sound of drums and the tramp of armed men were heard in the streets. The balconies were crowded with lovely women in gay attire to witness the military processions, and the Confederate flag in miniature was pinned on every bosom."

No one died in the Battle of Fort Sumter, but during the surrender ceremony, as banners flew and drums played, a powder keg accidentally exploded, killing one of Anderson's men and injuring several others. No one knew that he was the first of more than six hundred thousand soldiers to die in the long and bloody conflict.

CALL TO ARMS

After Anderson's surrender at Fort Sumter, the Confederacy doubled in size as other states seceded. Troubles flared on the border between North and South when pro-Southern citizens in Baltimore, Maryland— some of them rowdies nicknamed "plug-uglies"—tore down telegraph lines, burned bridges, and destroyed railroad tracks. Washington was cut off from the rest of the North, and guards volunteered to patrol the White House lawn and protect the president. The Confederacy's leaders, who wanted to make Lincoln even more nervous, moved the capital of the Confederacy to Richmond, Virginia, less than 150 miles from the White House.

Lincoln realized the situation was desperate. With less than sixteen thousand men in the entire federal army, most of them scattered across the country, the federal commander in chief knew he must raise an army to defend dozens of federal arsenals, forts, and naval yards. He needed manpower at once. When thousands of Confederate soldiers gathered at Harpers Ferry, Virginia, only a day's march away, Union politicians in Washington urged Lincoln to act. On April 15 the president called upon the volunteer soldiers who formed the state militias, thus rallying seventy-five thousand volunteers to the Union cause.

EYEWITNESS

"When William Cory came across the field . . . he was excited and said, 'Jonathan, the Rebs have fired upon and taken Fort Sumter.' Father got white and couldn't say a word. . . . After I had finished I went in to dinner. Mother said, 'What is the matter with Father?' He had gone right upstairs. I told her what we had heard. She went to him. After a while they came down. Father looked ten years older. Grandma wanted to know what was the trouble. Father told her and she began to cry. . . . She and mother were crying and I lit out for the barn. I do hate to see women cry."

THEODORE UPSON,
a sixteen-year-old in Indiana,
April 1861

SOUTH ATLANTIC BLOCKADE

Not only the army, but also the navy would be important to winning the war. Lincoln hoped to bring the South back into the Union without bloodshed. He wanted to use a naval blockade to surround the Confederacy and halt trade and travel. On April 19, 1861, Lincoln revealed his plan to prevent Southern ships from sailing. But the Confederates laughed, calling it a paper blockade because the U.S. Navy had only ninety ships, and the South had 3,500 miles of coastline! In fact, for the first months of war, nine out of ten Confederate vessels slipped safely through enemy lines.

The only thing worse than the Union navy was the Confederate navy! The South had few ships and even fewer sailors and guns for the ships. However, the Southern navy received a great boost when nearly a quarter of all the U.S. naval officers resigned to join the Confederacy.

Lincoln still believed in Union sea power and placed his faith in Secretary of the Navy Gideon Welles, whom he nicknamed "Father Neptune." Welles energetically recruited dozens of ships and crews for blockade duty. In less than

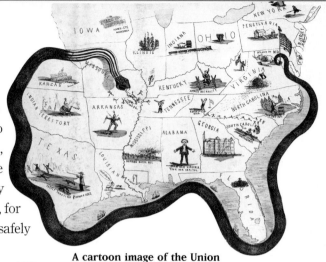

A cartoon image of the Union naval blockade.

The U.S. Navy was better equipped to fight the war at sea. Naval enlistees on the U.S.S. *Hunchback*, both black and white sailors, were experienced seamen, prepared for duty.

nine months, more than two hundred sixty warships were under Union command and a hundred more were on the drawing board or under construction.

The naval battle was waged not just at sea, but also on the rivers. Gunboats patrolled inland waters such as the Mississippi and Tennessee rivers, as well as the coastlines. Both North and South quickly realized that control of the waterways was important to military victory.

BUILDING A NAVY

During the four years of war, the Union was able to build its navy into a formidable force. There were only about 8,000 men in naval service in 1861, but by the close of the war, the U.S. Navy could claim 50,000 men. When the call went out, merchant marines volunteered, and all three of the upper classes at the U.S. Naval Academy enrolled in active service. Marines were installed on nearly every troop ship, mainly as guards to enforce orderly conduct in port and to prevent any desertion while sailors were docked.

American sailors were used to poor living conditions at sea, but the war imposed even heavier burdens on seamen. Especially disheartening to the average deckhand was the navy's elimination of a popular tradition: a daily ration of liquor. Four squadrons patrolled eastern waters to prevent Confederate commerce: The North Atlantic Squadron guarded Virginia and North Carolina, the South Atlantic Squadron covered the area from South Carolina to eastern Florida, the East Gulf Squadron sailed alongside southern and western Florida, and the West Indian Squadron was in charge of all other waters.

DID YOU KNOW?

Union naval inventor John Ericsson, a Swedish-born engineer, equipped one of his ships with a new invention he patented. Ericsson's flush toilet could work even below decks while most of the ship was underwater.

The Confederates did not have the industrial means to build enough of their own ships and were reduced to trying to purchase foreign boats for their navy and smuggle them in. The blockaded South effectively set mines in many harbors, using "stake torpedoes." These explosives angled up to catch the hulls of any passing ships. (*Torpedo* was the term used for what we call "mines" today.) Confederates also built small steam-driven, cigar-shaped vessels that they nicknamed "Davids," because the ships were up against the "Goliath" of the U.S. Navy. These smaller craft were submersibles, meaning that they took on enough water to lower their hulls below the waterline, leaving only a small amount of deck and a smokestack visible.

Both Confederate and Union ships carried heavy artillery, or guns. The most common weapons on shipboard were the 9-inch Dahlgrens, which could be mounted on pivots to give a wide arc of fire. The largest guns aboard were usually 15-inch mounted cannon.

Blockade-runners

During the war a hardy band of adventurers braved the dangers of Union patrols and earned fame as blockade-runners. In Margaret Mitchell's *Gone With the Wind*, the dashing character Rhett Butler is celebrated as a Confederate hero for his role in smuggling goods. He and others like him broke the Union blockade and transported goods in and out of the South. Many of these men were entrepreneurs risking danger for profit rather than glory because the rewards for success were enormous. For example, a captain might buy cotton for 6 cents a pound in the Confederacy, run the blockade, and then sell it to English buyers for 50 to 65 cents a pound.

Most runners could easily earn a profit of $50 per bale of cotton. Skippers were usually paid $5,000 a run, and deckhands earned as much as $250. None of these blockade-running ships were armed, and many were painted gunmetal gray to resemble Union vessels in case of patrols. Ships entering the Confederacy were loaded with boots, ladies' clothing, saddles, candles, quinine, and other goods, which were then sold at skyrocketing prices. As meat became more and more scarce, "Bermuda bacon"—imported pork from the island of Bermuda, which was a jumping-off point for many runners—was a rare delicacy enjoyed by those who could pay the steep price.

Both sides scrambled to organize armies and to train infantry (marching units), cavalry (horseback units) and artillery (cannon units). Many young men in the South had trained in local militias, and most young Southern men who had grown up in rural areas already knew how to hit a target with a rifle and ride a horse. These skills gave them a big advantage.

In the Union army, the federal government provided horses for its cavalry soldiers. The Confederacy usually expected men to bring their own trained horses to war—although the government would replace any horses killed in battle. Keeping the cavalry supplied with horses was a critical problem for both armies because the average cavalryman went through five horses a year. In just one battle-filled month, the Union army required more than seven thousand new horses for its cavalry corps.

Artillery batteries (soldiers who were gunners) were composed of four to six sizable weapons, such as Napoleons or Parrot guns. As guns became more accurate at longer distances, artillery became an important part of army tactics—the way soldiers fought battles.

Not everyone who joined the military was assigned to combat duty. On both sides there were thousands of clerks, hundreds of chaplains (ministers), and justices (known as judge advocates). Both armies had ordnance departments in charge of ammunition, arsenals, and armories; quartermaster departments to coordinate storage and transportation of uniforms and supplies; provost marshals to handle military police work; commissaries to handle food; a medical

MILITARY TERMS

Battalion: unit of 4 to 8 companies, 400 to 800 soldiers

Battery: artillery unit of 4 to 6 cannons

Brevet rank: temporary or honorary commission

Brigade: tactical unit of soldiers, 5 regiments, 5,000 soldiers

Color: a flag carried by a regiment

Company: 50 to 100 soldiers— 10 companies in a regiment

Corps: 2 or 3 divisions, totaling 30,000 to 45,000 men

Division: 2 or 3 brigades, totaling 10,000 to 15,000 men

Guidon: triangular or swallow-tailed flag carried by mounted command

Regiment: 500 to 1,000 soldiers

Squadron: in the cavalry, 2 companies, 100 to 200 soldiers

The Two Cabinets

Both President Lincoln and President Davis had difficulty finding leaders who could work together smoothly to form their cabinets—the advisors in charge of government departments. Aware of the deep divisions within his party, Lincoln offered four of his seven cabinet posts to Republican rivals: Edward Bates, Simon Cameron, William Seward, and Salmon Chase. Seward and Chase were such enemies that their quarrels were a big headache for Lincoln. He gave one post to a New Englander and another to a westerner; finally, to show his goodwill toward the border states, he offered the office of

postmaster general to a politician from Maryland. Despite their disputes, Lincoln's men got along a lot better than members of the Confederate cabinet.

During the war, Davis had to appoint not one, not two, but three secretaries of state—the cabinet member in charge of foreign and domestic policy. And the secretary of war post seemed even more of a revolving door; Davis had to appoint six men in a row, because he constantly overruled his advisors. One of Davis's most skilled advisors, Judah P. Benjamin, was first appointed attorney general, then secretary of war, and finally secretary of state.

Camp life for most soldiers was a waiting game. Men often played cards or did domestic chores between long hours on guard duty or the drilling field, anticipating the battles ahead. Brothers and friends tried to join the same company to relieve the tedium of life in the ranks.

corps; a signal corps to perform flag and torch signaling; and finally a corps of engineers to design and build forts, bridges, and roads. Both armies needed cooks and other labor to organize the care and feeding of the soldiers.

The Confederates also established a torpedo bureau to build land mines and a niter and mining bureau to collect coal, lead, iron, and saltpeter for making ammunition. In Southern cities, these men even supervised the collection of human waste from chamber pots for fertilizer to help make nitrate. A soldier's life was far from glamorous!

RECRUITING SONG

"I want to be a soldier,
And with the soldier stand,
A knapsack on my shoulder,
A musket in my hand.
And there beside Jeff Davis
So glorious and brave,
I'll whip the cussed Yankee,
And drive him to his grave."

Men on each side of the Mason-Dixon line felt their side was better equipped to win a war. Southerners believed they had a stronger chance of winning because of their patriotism and defensive military position. They wanted to build a wall around the South to keep the Yankees out.

The federals were convinced that they had the industrial might to triumph in a war. The North produced nearly all the nation's manufactured, or machine-made, goods and had six times more factories than the South. New York State alone manufactured four times the value of goods produced by the entire Confederacy. One county in Connecticut produced more firearms than all the Southern states combined! The North boasted 22,000 miles of railroad track to the South's 9,000, and 96 percent of American trains were manufactured in the North. The North had more and better ports and canals.

Finally, the North had a larger population, more than 20 million; the South's population of 9 million included more than 3.5 million slaves. Although Northerners believed that their material advantages would insure victory, they did not realize just how determined Confederates were to obtain their independence.

Soldiers risked their lives, and these veterans of battle sacrificed limbs, during their Civil War service.

The Sanitary Commission

In April 1861 more than three thousand New Yorkers turned out to rally to the Union cause and form a huge relief society that would provide bandages, clothing, and other supplies for the soldiers at the front. All across the North, hundreds of these networks and organizations became loosely linked in what was known as the Sanitary Commission. Many of these groups held "Sanitary Fairs," auctions and sales to raise money for the Union cause. A two-week fund-raiser in Chicago brought nearly $100,000 to the Union treasury.

Hundreds of women volunteered to become nurses, although nursing had been a male occupation before the war. After she became the Superintendent of Nurses, Dorothea Dix demanded that volunteers be over thirty and "plain in appearance," rules that earned her the nickname "Dragon Dix." But her skilled and efficient nurses boosted her reputation throughout the Union. Nurse Mary Anne Bickerdyke wore her Quaker bonnet as she sought to comfort wounded men close to battlefields. She didn't wait for men to be transported to hospitals but went out to the field, braving danger so soldiers wouldn't die before getting the medical care they needed.

More than three thousand women served as nurses, officially and unofficially, during the course

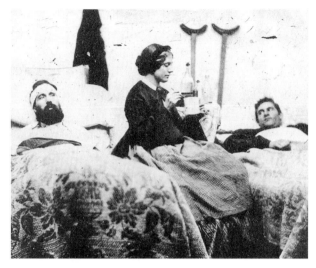
Union nurse caring for wounded soldiers.

of the war. One of these was Louisa May Alcott, who spent time in a Washington hospital before she returned home to Concord, Massachusetts, to write her first book, *Hospital Sketches,* and then *Little Women.* This fictionalized story of her family during and after the Civil War became an American classic.

Disease—even illnesses like measles—killed more men in the army than wounds received in battle, and a Sanitary Commission supervisor, Frederick Law Olmsted, praised women volunteers: "God knows what we should have done without them; they have worked like heroes night and day."

Clara Barton

When the Civil War began, Clara Barton was living in Washington, D.C., and working in the U.S. Patent Office. She went home to her native Massachusetts to organize relief efforts to help the soldiers. She coordinated donations and enlisted volunteers to form an independent nursing corps. Instead of waiting for the wounded to come to government hospitals, she took oxcarts of supplies to the front. She raised thousands of dollars and nursed thousands of men. Near the end of the war, Barton spent time and money trying to reunite families with loved ones. She received more than sixty thousand letters from families seeking information about prisoners of war and other missing soldiers. Clara Barton went on to become the founder of the American Red Cross.

MANASSAS JUNCTION, JULY 21: The ladies had packed the picnic baskets with excitement and care. Hoping to witness a Union victory and to cheer on the federal soldiers, Washington sightseers decided to ride out to Manassas Junction. Instead, in the heat of battle, Yankee soldiers in blue were the first to abandon the field. The Union troops broke ranks and in haste and confusion beat a retreat. The scene was so jumbled that many civilians were swept away in the stampede of soldiers fleeing back toward Washington. Panic had spread among the Northern soldiers when they were overrun by the Southern enemy charging forward while bellowing their Rebel yells, a bloodcurdling sound that terrified those who heard it.

Colonel Robert E. Lee, a U.S. Army veteran but also a loyal Virginian, had refused Lincoln's offer to command the Union army and instead became Davis's chief military advisor. Lee knew that this first encounter with the Yankees near a stream known as Bull Run, just 25

miles southwest of Washington, would be important. But even Lee did not realize how crucial this battle would become until after the two forces locked horns outside the tiny railroad junction on a muggy July morning.

The hero of Fort Sumter, Confederate General P. G. T. Beauregard, commanded twenty thousand men. The general learned from spies that the Union commander General Irvin McDowell, a West Point classmate of Beauregard's, planned to strike with his force of thirty-seven thousand. Beauregard requested help, and Confederate General Joseph E. Johnston, who was camped in the Shenandoah Valley, responded at once. Johnston came to the rescue by shipping ten thousand troops by train—the first time in history the railroad was used to deliver soldiers to a battlefield. After Johnston's men arrived, the Yankees were soundly beaten.

During the battle Confederate Brigadier General Thomas J. Jackson and his brigade of volunteers, some of them cadets from the Virginian Military Institute in their pressed gray uniforms, remained calm. Jackson's soldiers stood so steadfast while bullets swirled around them that the general earned the nickname "Stonewall."

Young volunteers from the First Virginia Militia, known as the "Richmond Grays," enlisted as soon as they could convince the recruiting agents they were eighteen—the age limit for soldiers—or secure a parent's signature. Over 60 percent of the soldiers in both armies were under the age of twenty-five.

Troops of the Union commander McDowell staggered back to Washington, in disgrace and defeat. Realizing that he must find a better military leader, Lincoln eventually selected the young Mexican War hero General George McClellan to head the newly organized Army of the Potomac.

BATTLE IN MISSOURI

WILSON'S CREEK, AUGUST 10: The struggle for the West (which today we call the Midwest) was very important, especially during the early months of battle, when Lincoln needed to hold the sprawling Union together. Missouri, which contained several major river systems and rich natural resources, was a key state. When the pro-Confederate governor tried to seize the St. Louis arsenal after the fall of Fort Sumter, a loyal army officer, Captain Nathaniel Lyon, smuggled federal guns and ammunition to safety, carrying them to a fort in Illinois.

Promoted to the rank of general, Lyon led six thousand Yankee troops to southwestern Missouri to try to scare away Rebel units in the area. Even when he discovered that he faced a force more than twice the size of his, he refused to back down. This plucky Union general launched a sneak attack and smoke filled the air as ferocious fighting erupted. Lyon was shot twice before a third bullet killed him. His men were driven away shortly after. The battle lasted less than six hours and cost the lives of 15 percent of all participants. This was a very high mortality rate (the number who died compared with those who survived).

Lyon's defeat would have been even worse for the Union if the Confederates had captured retreating Yankees. But luckily the Rebels collapsed after the day's victory and did not give chase, a costly mistake. Most of Missouri remained in Union control for the rest of the war.

BATTLES AT-A-GLANCE

FIRST BATTLE OF BULL RUN
Manassas Junction, Virginia, July 21

Union troops: 37,000
Confederate troops: 35,000

Union casualties: 2,896
Confederate casualties: 1,982
CONFEDERATE VICTORY

BATTLE OF WILSON'S CREEK
Missouri, August 10

Union troops: 5,400
Confederate troops: 11,000

Union casualties: 1,131
Confederate casualties: 1,130
CONFEDERATE VICTORY

Mary Chesnut's Diary

[JULY 22, 1861] *"Mrs. Davis came in so softly that I did not know she was here until she leaned over me and said: 'A great battle has been fought. Joe Johnston led the right wing, and Beauregard the left wing of the army. Your husband is all right. Wade Hampton is wounded.'. . . We had been such anxious wretches."*

Mary Boykin Chesnut was the wife of South Carolina Senator James Chesnut, Jr., the first federal legislator to resign after secession. She recorded her thoughts and feelings about the war in her diary. She was in Charleston during the bombardment of Fort Sumter, in Alabama for the Confederate inauguration, and often in Richmond as a frequent guest at the Confederate White House, the home of her good friends President Jefferson Davis and his wife, Varina. Chesnut's journal took on a melancholy tone following the Battle of Bull Run, when the war became real for women as the funerals began. Her writing reflected Confederate hopes and defeat. She hoped to publish the diary herself, but the manuscript was published only after her death and remains one of the most important records of life in the Confederacy.

In late April 1861, within a week of the attack on Fort Sumter, Northern blacks rallied to the Union cause in Pittsburgh, Pennsylvania, where they formed an independent military unit, the Hannibal Guards. The next week the secretary of war received a note from a black man in Washington who offered himself and boasted, "I can be found about the Senate Chambers, as I have been employed about the premises for some years." This patriot further confided that he knew "three hundred reliable colored citizens" willing to defend the capital.

Independent black volunteer drill companies in Cleveland, Boston, and throughout the North wanted to respond to war fever. African Americans knew they had more at stake than most white Americans in the fight to keep the South within the Union.

Instead of being lauded for their patriotism, black volunteers all too often faced indifference, discrimination, and suspicion. Even many ardent abolitionists were hesitant to support black soldiers because they feared if the blacks lost their nerve in the heat of battle, it would damage the cause of racial equality.

Lincoln and his advisors opposed blacks in the military, even though some Union commanders were sympathetic to the idea of using African Americans within Union army camps. The President's initial opposition was a major stumbling block for African Americans seeking equality and a role in the war.

Still, many black men seized the initiative and organized in military units on their own, establishing volunteer groups in Kansas and behind enemy lines in South Carolina.

Within weeks of the First Battle of Bull Run in July 1861, Union commanders faced a dilemma even more perplexing than recovering from that defeat. By the hundreds and thousands, slaves were escaping behind Northern lines. The problem was handled on an *ad hoc,* or case-by-case, basis during the first chaotic months of war. This inconsistent policy caused bitter confusion, especially for slaves seeking safety. Some Union officers gave runaway slaves refuge, and others simply let slave owners come and reclaim their slave property. In the first summer of war, many African Americans who tried to join the Union cause

Harriet Tubman

Harriet Tubman was one of eleven children born to her slave parents on a plantation in Maryland. While she was still a girl, an overseer threw a lead weight at her head, knocking her unconscious. She finally recovered, but the blow left a scar on her head. From that day forward, she was committed to seeking freedom for herself and her fellow slaves. When her master finally died, twenty-nine-year-old Tubman decided to escape to avoid being sold. She left her family and made her way to Philadelphia, where she became active in the abolitionist movement. Tubman was willing to break the law to free her fellow slaves, and she was nicknamed "General Tubman" during her service as a "conductor" on the Underground Railroad. When the Civil War began, Tubman volunteered for Union service at Fort Monroe in Virginia and was then transferred to Beaufort, South Carolina, where she helped Yankee commanders liberate slaves on Confederate plantations. She also served as a spy for the Union cause.

were returned to slavery by the very soldiers in blue whom they had hoped would protect them.

The Reverend Sella Martin of the Joy Street Baptist Church in Boston, a former slave who had made his way to freedom in 1855, spoke out against Union commanders who returned runaways to their masters. Martin warned that aiding slave owners would make "the slaves determined to fight for the South, in the hope that their masters may set them free after the war." Finally, the federal government stepped in.

On August 6, 1861, Congress passed the First Confiscation Act, which required the seizure of all property in aid of rebellion—including human property, slaves. Rapidly, Union quartermasters and engineers put the African-American refugees to work as manual laborers—ditchdiggers and dike builders. Ex-slave women were drafted into roles of cooks and washerwomen. The war was less than six months old, but an increasingly black labor force was demonstrating its vitality to the Union.

Frederick Douglass urged that African Americans be permitted to enlist and fight. His dream was fulfilled in 1863 by over 180,000 blacks in Union uniforms.

CAPTURE OF PORT ROYAL, SOUTH CAROLINA
NOVEMBER 7, UNION VICTORY

The artillery shells were flying. Union gunboats were trying to destroy Southern ports along the Carolina coast to cut off the Confederacy from the outside world. A rain of shells bombarded the harbors. On August 29 the Union navy captured Fort Hatteras, near Albemarle Sound in North Carolina. Then Union Flag Officer Samuel F. DuPont set his sights on Port Royal, South Carolina, located halfway between the North Carolina border and Savannah, Georgia. Steaming out of Hampton Roads, Virginia, with twelve hundred men on board, DuPont arrived at Port Royal Sound and began to attack the twin battlements guarding the sound. After four hours of brutal shelling, one fort was abandoned and the other surrendered. When the Yankee troops poured into the area, they discovered that planters on the nearby islands of Hilton Head, St. Helena, Parris, Phillips, and Daw had abandoned their plantations, leaving thousands of African Americans behind. These men and women were eager to assist the conquering Union force.

Enslaved African Americans of all ages saw the Civil War as an opportunity for freedom. Both men and women sought to escape their masters when the Union army was nearby.

The Union military officers called African-American refugees (slaves who fled behind enemy lines) "contrabands" (confiscated property), and employed them as stablehands, cooks, and laborers to help the Union army. They did not want to return slaves to Southern owners, but they also did not want to upset slave owners in the Union's border states. Politicians in Washington were unsure how to handle this tricky situation.

NEW YEAR'S RESOLUTIONS

The first encounters between North and South convinced Confederate commanders that the war would be over soon. A string of Confederate military victories and Yankee battlefield blunders fueled Southern overconfidence. Jefferson Davis hoped for a quick settlement because he wanted to secure the glory of Confederate independence. But his brand-new government faced several problems. The Confederacy had to establish a whole new government while trying to launch a major military offensive and protect itself from Yankee invasion as well. Despite the competing demands pulling his new nation in several different directions, Davis hoped to bring all white Southerners together in a show of patriotic unity.

By year's end, Abraham Lincoln was in despair. He had not even wanted a war, and now the Southern states seemed likely to slip away. He grew more and more worried as Union generals, well stocked with supplies and men, seemed in no hurry to lead men into battle. Lincoln kept urging his officers to take action, but they seemed content to postpone seizing the initiative indefinitely. The Union president told one of his friends, "Delay is ruining us." From the banks of the Mississippi to the shores of the Potomac River, the Union command had dug in for the winter, anchored to army campsites. Lincoln grew more and more grim as his commanders still held back, unwilling to lure the enemy into combat.

Both presidents wanted to bring the other side to the table to negotiate a peace and end the war quickly, but instead they were forced to place their faith in their generals. Both sought to conquer the enemy on the battleground, and prayed for victory.

EYEWITNESS

"One of the first things that I 'members was my pappy waking me up in the middle of the night, dressin' me in the dark, all the time telling me to keep quiet. One of the twins hollered some an' pappy put his hand over its mouth to keep it quiet. After we was dressed, he went outside and peeped round for a minute, then he comed back an' got us. We snook out of the house an' long de woods path. Pappy toted one of the twins and holding me by the han' an' mammy carrying the other two. I reckon that I will always 'member that walk, with the bushes slapping my legs, with the wind sighin' in the trees, and the hoot owls and whippoorwills hollering at each other from the big trees. I was half asleep an' skeered stiff, but in a little while we passed the plum thicket an' there were the mules and wagon. . . ."

MARY BARBOUR,
a former slave recalling her family's escape to the Union army

CHAPTER 3

1862

As the Confederacy celebrated its first birthday, the Union mourned the past twelve months of war and the promise of more to come. In his second year in command, Jefferson Davis was encouraged by the military success of his two top generals, Stonewall Jackson and Robert E. Lee. He watched their progress like a doting father, noting that Jackson seemed unbeatable during his encounters with the Yankee army and Lee used brilliant strategy in battle after battle. Once Lee was promoted to army command, the hopes and dreams of the proud Confederate nation rested with him.

During this period of great expectations for the Confederacy, the Union leader was in despair. Worry and care weighed Lincoln down, as his tired, thinning face showed his presidential responsibilities. Only the rise of an obscure military figure in the West, Ulysses S. Grant, gave Lincoln any hope at all. In November he replaced George McClellan, the popular but unsuccessful commander of the largest Eastern army, with another general, Ambrose Burnside. None of Lincoln's commanders except Grant, however, seemed able to snare victory from the hard-fighting Rebel armies.

THE YEAR AT-A-GLANCE

March 9
Showdown at Hampton Roads
(*Monitor* vs. *Merrimack*)
Hampton Roads, Virginia

April 6–7
Battle of Shiloh
Shiloh Church, Tennessee

August 28–30
Second Battle of Bull Run
Manassas Junction, Virginia

September 17
Battle of Antietam
Sharpsburg, Maryland

December 13
Battle of Fredericksburg
Fredericksburg, Virginia

Union troops gathered near Cumberland Landing, Virginia, planning to march on the Confederate capital of Richmond.

BATTLES IN TENNESSEE:
FORT HENRY AND FORT DONELSON,
FEBRUARY 6–16, UNION VICTORY

GENERAL ULYSSES S. GRANT

Southern soldiers at Fort Henry stood guard along the Tennessee River, the gateway to Kentucky. This spot was important because river traffic on the waterway linked the two halves of the Confederacy—the upper South and the deep South. Union General Ulysses S. Grant knew the river was the main supply route for the Southern army, so he and his force of fifteen thousand (including seven federal gunboats) bombarded the Rebels and won.

The fall of Fort Henry caused the remaining Confederate troops in the area to race back toward Fort Donelson to prevent its capture. A winter storm derailed Grant's plans of swift victory at Fort Donelson and for two days Northern men in blue and Southern soldiers in gray fought fiercely. Finally, on February 16, the Union army was victorious. Confederates were forced to accept Grant's harsh terms for "immediate and unconditional" surrender, and Grant earned the nickname "Unconditional Surrender" (like his initials, U. S.) Grant. This stunning twin triumph in Tennessee was the Union's first major military success.

WAR IN THE FAR WEST

Although most of the fighting in the Civil War occurred east of the Mississippi, the blue and the gray clashed in the far West as well. Confederate General Henry Sibley decided to stir up some trouble near San Antonio, Texas, where he recruited a force of nearly four thousand troops, mostly Texans, tough horsemen known as the Texas Rangers. These rangers moved west along the Rio Grande until Union forces met them at Val Verde. In a hard battle, the federal soldiers were forced to retreat.

Next General Sibley led his men northward toward Santa Fe, New Mexico. When Union troops from Colorado tried to block the Confederates, the two forces fought at Glorieta Pass, New Mexico, on March 27. The eager "Pikes Peakers," as the raw Colorado recruits were known, threw themselves into a blistering battle where smoke and gunpowder filled the air. A small detachment of Union soldiers sneaked around behind the battle lines to steal Confederate supply wagons and force the Texas Rangers to turn back. This battle eventually became known as the "Gettysburg of the West" and ended Confederate dreams of conquest west of the Mississippi River.

BATTLE AT-A-GLANCE

BATTLE OF SHILOH
Shiloh Church, Tennessee,
April 6–7

Union troops: 65,000
Confederate troops: 40,000

Union casualties: 13,000
Confederate casualties: 10,500
UNION VICTORY

Showdown

THE *MONITOR* VS. *MERRIMACK*
HAMPTON ROADS, VIRGINIA
MARCH 9
DRAW

Turret of the ironclad *Monitor*

This clash at Hampton Roads was the first sea battle using "ironclads," wooden ships covered in metal armor for ramming strength and defensive protection. Although neither side could claim victory, this encounter showed that wooden ships were no longer any match for the odd-looking but effective ironclads.

When they abandoned the shipyards at Norfolk, Virginia, the Union troops sank all the ships left behind. The Confederacy raised a warship called the *Merrimack* from the depths of the Norfolk harbor, rebuilt her, and covered her in heavy iron armament. Renamed the C.S.S. *Virginia* and relaunched off Hampton Roads on March 8, the *Merrimack* was determined to break through the Union blockade. She encountered a flotilla of Union ships, sank two and fired on the others. The next day the *Monitor*, the Union's prize ironclad, steamed into the harbor to take on the *Merrimack*. Although the battle between these two ships was technically considered a draw, the clash of the "invincible" ironclads was a spectacular sight. In the end, neither the *Merrimack* nor the *Monitor* survived the war. The Rebels blew up their prize ironclad rather than let her fall into Union hands. Months later the *Monitor* was lost in a storm at sea.

BATTLE OF SHILOH

Shiloh Church was a quiet spot until the Confederates made a surprise attack on the Union army camped nearby. General Ulysses S. Grant and his troops had stopped at Shiloh Church to wait for reinforcements before trying to capture Corinth, a town and important railway station in northeast Mississippi that connected the western Confederacy with headquarters in Virginia.

Yankee soldiers were cooking their breakfast when they heard the terrifying sound of the Rebel yell. Confederate General Albert Sidney Johnston launched a surprise attack and nearly pushed the Union troops into the Tennessee River. During the battle's earliest hours, Johnston was wounded in the leg and bled to death before medical help could arrive. A long night of rain and the arrival of Union reinforcements gave U. S. Grant the opportunity he needed to prepare for battle the next morning.

The two armies fought ferociously the next day, until the Confederates, now commanded by P. G. T. Beauregard, reluctantly withdrew. In telegrams back to Richmond, Beauregard had prematurely declared the battle a victory, so the defeat was doubly humiliating for the retreating Rebels. The fierce and bloody nature of the Shiloh encounter, with its huge death toll and combined casualties of nearly twenty-five thousand, taught Grant and his friend and division commander, General William T. Sherman, a terrible lesson about war. They could never underestimate the South's determination to win. It would not be a short or fair war.

EYEWITNESS

"*I write you a few lines to inform you of the times. Hugh has got the measles. He has been complaining two or three days. I have just returned from the hospital where I have been to carry him—distance from camp half mile. . . . There was twelve of us at first. There is but six now able for duty. Four has the measles, one has the chills, one the typhoid newmonia. . . .*"

D. C. JONES,
a teenager who joined up with
the Texas Rangers

The Union kept a close eye on New Orleans, Louisiana, the link between the Mississippi River and the open sea. Protected by several forts, this port city near the Gulf of Mexico was the wealthiest Confederate stronghold in the Delta region. Bales of cotton, boxes of arms and ammunition, and tons of other goods were stored in warehouses near its busy docks. In late April the formidable Union naval commodore, David Farragut, decided the time was right to attack New Orleans. He sailed his large fleet of ships past the forts protecting the city and battled his way through to capture New Orleans.

The outnumbered Confederate forces set fire to fifteen thousand bales of cotton, several steamboats, and millions of dollars worth of supplies to keep them out of Union hands.

The white citizens of New Orleans created enormous obstacles for Union General Benjamin Butler and his army of occupation. When the Union navy lowered the Louisiana flag to hoist Old Glory, the Union flag, civilians fought back. Southern ladies were disrespectful toward the Union, some even reportedly spitting on men in federal uniform. Butler retaliated by allowing his men to arrest any Southern woman who insulted his soldiers. The outraged people of New Orleans nicknamed the general "Beast" Butler. The Union stranglehold on New Orleans, at the mouth of the Mississippi, gave the Union navy the launching pad it needed: From there, Union gunboats worked their way up the river to capture Baton Rouge, Louisiana, and Natchez, Mississippi. Both cities surrendered without much of a fight. Only Vicksburg, Mississipi, and Port Hudson, Louisiana, remained under Confederate control.

EYEWITNESS

"*Several days after the Federal Army evacuated Baton Rouge we ventured to enter the gates of our sweet little city. . . . No words can tell the scene that those deserted rooms presented. The grand portraits . . . slashed by swords clear across from side to side, stabbed and mutilated in every brutal way! The contents of closets had been poured over the floors; molasses and vinegar and everything that defaces and stains had been smeared over the walls and furniture. . . .*"

ELIZA RIPLEY,
describing Baton Rouge,
Louisiana, in 1862

A mosquito fleet of a dozen small Confederate gunboats was soundly defeated by Farragut's superior force at the Battle of New Orleans.

Children and the Military

Nearly 5 percent of the soldiers fighting during the Civil War were younger than eighteen, the legal age for recruits. Many lied about their age to join the army. Drummer boys ten to twelve years old could be found with troops in both armies, and even younger boys volunteered to serve on warships. Carrying gunpowder to the men firing cannon during battle, the children were nicknamed "powder monkeys." These shipboard volunteers had to scramble quickly down the narrow ship ladders to where the powder was stored and reappear rapidly to keep the cannon booming. Both powder monkeys and drummer boys, many of them orphans, went on to enlist in the armed forces.

Young recruits were welcomed into the ranks as powder monkeys.

Very young girls, too, were found in army camps. When a male relative joined up, a handful of girls accompanied troops, who adopted them as mascots. They were known as "daughters of the regiment" or "vivandières." Sarah Taylor accompanied her Southern relatives with the Confederacy's 1st Tennessee Regiment, and Lucy Ann Cox was adopted by the 13th Virginia Regiment. These fresh-faced young girls fueled the spirit of patriotism of men marching into battle. Few of these girls ever went into battle, but Marie Tepe, or "French Mary" as she was known, was wounded serving as vivandière of the 114th Pennsylvania.

Pets in Camp

Troops on both sides adopted animals along the way. B. F. Taylor, a journalist from the *Chicago Tribune* who traveled with the Union army, described the pets—many unusual—that he saw: "They have the strangest pets in the army, that nobody would dream of 'taking to' at home. . . . One of the boys has carried a red squirrel, through 'thick and thin,' over a thousand miles. . . . Another's affections overflow upon a slow-winking, unspeculative little owl. . . . A third gives his heart to a young Cumberland Mountain bear. But chief among camp pets are dogs. Riding on the saddle bow, tucked into a baggage-wagon, mounted on a knapsack, growling under a gun, are dogs. . . . There was one in an Illinois regiment, and I rather think regarded as belonging to it, though his name may not be on the muster roll. He has

On rare occasions, a soldier's family might make a visit to his camp. Usually only officers were granted this privilege.

been under fire and twice wounded, and left the tip of his tail at the battle of Stones River." When they went home on leave or retired from the army, soldiers often took their pets with them.

BATTLE OF SEVEN PINES

In July 1861, when Lincoln appointed thirty-four-year-old George B. McClellan head of the North's principal field army, McClellan had an air of success about him. He was a good organizer who was popular with the troops. By the following spring, this air had evaporated and his commander in chief, President Lincoln, was impatient with his constant stalling. McClellan had gotten no closer to Richmond and seemed more concerned with drilling his troops than actually engaging in battle.

As summer approached, McClellan shipped ninety thousand soldiers by boat to Fort Monroe on the Virginia Peninsula. The plan was to march northward from there toward the Confederate capital at Richmond. After covering only 15 miles, McClellan's force got bogged down for more than a month until the Confederates finally evacuated on May 4.

GENERAL GEORGE B. McCLELLAN

Meanwhile, Confederate General Joseph Johnston made good use of this time, digging in an impressive defensive line near Seven Pines, five miles east of Richmond. When McClellan's men arrived, Johnston attacked; they fought for two days, but neither side could claim victory.

Because General Johnston was severely wounded at Seven Pines, Jefferson Davis appointed General Robert E. Lee to take his place. In the weeks ahead, Lee's skill as commander of the Southern armies further threatened McClellan, whose military abilities did not seem up to the challenge.

JACKSON'S SHENANDOAH CAMPAIGN

"Defend the valley!" Lee told Jackson in the spring of 1862, and defend it he did. Lying between the Blue Ridge Mountains and the Alleghenies, the rich and fertile lands of the Shenandoah Valley, the breadbasket of the Confederacy, were threatened by Union invaders.

Confederate General Thomas "Stonewall" Jackson's discipline had already made him legendary. When he was offered an alcoholic drink following battle, Jackson replied, "Colonel do you know why I habitually abstain from intoxicating liquors? Because I like the taste of them, and when I discovered that to be the case, I made up my

BATTLES AT-A-GLANCE

BATTLE OF SEVEN PINES
Fair Oaks Station, Virginia,
May 31–June 1

Union troops: 100,000
Confederate troops: 65,000

Union casualties: 5,000
Confederate casualties: 6,100
DRAW

JACKSON'S SHENANDOAH CAMPAIGN
Shenandoah Valley, Virginia
March 23–June 9
CONFEDERATE VICTORIES

GENERAL ROBERT E. LEE

Photographers often went to the battlefields to capture images of soldiers at the front—such as this portrait of the Union artillery batteries near Seven Pines.

mind at once to do without them." His strong will and iron determination made him an awesome soldier, worshipped by his own troops and feared by the enemy.

In just over a month, Jackson clashed with federal troops at almost a dozen Virginia towns, claiming victory after victory. Though Jackson's force was much smaller than the Union's, his troops were able to bob and weave, thrust and parry, to drive the superior Union forces back.

Between battles Jackson advised his officers, "Always mystify, mislead, and surprise the enemy, if possible. And when you strike and overcome him, never let up in the pursuit so long as your men have strength to follow. . . ." Over the course of his bold campaign, Jackson lost only twenty-five hundred men, but the federals had seven thousand casualties. Jackson's force, which never swelled to more than seventeen thousand, kept the Union army, numbering more than fifty thousand, on the run.

GENERAL STONEWALL JACKSON

THE SEVEN DAYS' BATTLES
VIRGINIA PENINSULA

Yanks and Rebs filled the air with gunpowder and smoke and littered the countryside with corpses during a weeklong series of battles on the distant outskirts of Richmond. Union troops under McClellan launched an opening attack at Oak Grove on June 25. The next day, when Lee's Confederates attacked at Mechanicsville, their charge stalled. When the Confederates struck again at Gaines' Mill, after a day-long battle Lee's boldness paid off, as his sixty thousand men broke through the center of the Union line and sent Yankee forces sprawling. But Confederate losses were high.

Lee inflicted more damage in encounters at Savage Station and Glendale as the federals retreated, culminating in a tremendous slaughter at Malvern Hill on July 1. More than five thousand attacking Confederates fell on the slopes of the hill alone. An eyewitness described the carnage, "A third of them were dead or dying, but enough of them were alive and moving to give the field a . . . crawling effect." Many Southern troops had fallen, but the Yankees were temporarily beaten back, and the threat to Richmond, for the moment, was over. Though he suffered tremendous losses, Lee saved the Confederate capital. McClellan's army was soon recalled to Washington and many of the men turned over to General Pope.

BATTLES AT-A-GLANCE

THE SEVEN DAYS' BATTLES
Virginia Peninsula,
June 25–August 1

Union troops: 115,000
Confederate troops: 92,000

Union casualties: 15,800
Confederate casualties: 20,100
CONFEDERATE VICTORY

SECOND BATTLE OF BULL RUN
Manassas Junction, Virginia,
August 28–30

Union troops: 75,000
Confederate troops: 48,500

Union casualties: 16,000
Confederate casualties: 9,100
CONFEDERATE VICTORY

Sometimes the battles came so near that children at play, like these youngsters at Sudley Ford near Bull Run, might see soldiers marching off to war.

Union soldiers stockpiled cannonballs at Yorktown, Virginia, for the battles ahead.

SECOND BATTLE OF BULL RUN
MANASSAS JUNCTION, VIRGINIA

Scorching heat and memories of Confederate victory the year before on the same battlefield tormented Union troops when they faced the enemy near Bull Run in the summer of 1862. Union General John Pope bragged that he would seek revenge and not only defeat the Confederate military, but "whip" Southern civilians into submission as well.

Confederate General Stonewall Jackson struck the first blow, near Cedar Mountain on August 9. After a hard fight in 100-degree heat, Jackson defeated the federal forces of General Nathaniel Banks. Lee's cavalry commander, J.E.B. Stuart, humiliated Pope by swooping down on the Union headquarters and capturing a case containing more than $300,000—nearly $5,000,000 in today's money—and the general's dress uniform.

On August 28, Pope discovered Jackson and his troops lying in wait on the killing fields of Bull Run. Unfortunately, the Union general delayed his main attack until the next day. Lee and Longstreet, on their way with thirty thousand reinforcements, joined Jackson in time to defeat the Yankees at Manassas again. Confederate forces drove Pope back to the defensive lines encircling Washington. Lincoln relieved Pope of his command and reluctantly appointed George McClellan, once again, as head of the Union forces at Washington.

Women Soldiers

In the summer of 1862, twenty-one-year-old Sarah Rosetta Wakeman decided to leave her home in upstate New York, disguise herself as a man, and enlist in the army. She assumed a false identity as Private

KADY BROWNELL— ONE WOMAN IN UNIFORM.

Lyon Wakeman and served with the 153rd New York Regiment. The army was so desperate for soldiers that few recruiting officers bothered with physical exams and took anyone who looked able-bodied. She served in the Red River campaign in Louisiana, and only her wartime death revealed that she had been a woman.

We have no idea how many other women dressed in men's clothing during wartime and played a role as soldiers. Information is scarce, but there have been more than a hundred documented cases.

Women went to war for a variety of reasons. Scores were accompanying sweethearts and husbands or searching for loved ones. Some were simply independent spirits, unwilling to obey society's rules and wait out the war.

A few of the women who successfully assumed a male identity published memoirs about their wartime adventures. Sarah Emma Edmonds wrote *Nurse and Spy in the Union Army*, describing her contributions to the Union cause as "Frank Thompson." Another account, *The Woman in Battle*, told the story of "Lieutenant Henry Buford," who raised a Confederate cavalry company and was wounded twice in battle.

"If we are defeated, it will be by the people at home," an Atlanta newspaper warned when war broke out. Both the North and the South required a strong economy to support the war effort, and both sides relied on the industry and labor of those left behind to support the soldiers at the front.

Not only did women on the home front have to keep the "home fires burning," but they were expected to chop the wood as well! They often had to learn to handle an ax, a plow, a pitchfork, even a gun to keep family farms running. The army required enormous amounts of food, so farmers were expected to raise extra crops and sell them to the government to supply the armies with food.

In the South, especially, producing enough food was a considerable challenge. Confederate leaders warned planters they could "plant corn and be free or plant cotton and be whipped." Cotton production was cut in half in the war's first year as Southern farmers planted beans and corn, vegetables and grain, to keep the Confederacy fed. But poor harvests and other handicaps plagued the Southern farmer.

In the North farm production accelerated, and sales of farm machinery such as reapers tripled in response to the increased demand. Good harvests doubled the export of foodstuffs to Europe. Because of the cotton blockade, Northern farmers turned to wool for clothing, and the sheep population rose from 15 million to 32 million. The number of sewing machines in use doubled between 1861 and 1865.

Although more than three thousand companies in the North failed in the first twelve months of war, the economy soon bounced back, and businesses

DID YOU KNOW?

During the Seven Days' Battles, when the Yankees used hydrogen balloons for observation, Confederate General James Longstreet expressed a wish that the South had a balloon. Scores of patriotic Virginia women donated hundreds of ball gowns and sewed a patchwork Rebel balloon, which Longstreet called the "Last Silk Dress in the Confederacy." Although captured by the Yankees after its maiden flight, the balloon symbolized the loyalty of Confederate women.

Southern women sewing near Cedar Mountain, Virginia.

began to grow and prosper. In Philadelphia, for example, fifty-eight new factories opened in 1862, fifty-seven in 1863, and sixty-three in 1864.

While production grew in the North, the South faced shortages and deprivation. Hemmed in by the blockade and unable to export or import products, Confederates celebrated the ethic of self-sacrifice. Southern matrons gave "starvation parties," where only water was served to guests. Desperate times produced desperate measures, and many Southerners gave up family jewels and silver for Confederate bonds. One Alabama woman urged her sister Confederates to sell their hair to European wigmakers and donate the proceeds to the Confederacy.

Increasingly, Southern households found it difficult to feed their families. Women left on the plantations struggled, and wives left behind on small farms in the rural South were especially hard hit. Stripped of husbands, sons, mules, tools, and firearms, they strove wearily on.

Some women tried to smuggle boots for their menfolk through the picket lines by wearing them under their long skirts.

The First Ladies

Neither Mary Todd Lincoln nor Varina Howell Davis expected to find joy in her role as first lady for a wartime president. Each was overwhelmed by the burdens associated with her husband's office and completely loyal to her husband's cause. Each endured harsh criticism for her personality, and each woman suffered great personal tragedy during her time in the White House.

In contrast to her more serious husband, Mary Todd Lincoln was a vivacious and colorful addition to the Washington scene. She was talkative and outgoing, while Lincoln reserved his humor for a circle of close friends. Though she was gaudy and enjoyed fashion (her collection of shoes became the subject of public gossip), her husband often appeared in public in worn or mismatched clothing. But the Lincolns shared a passion for their sons—Robert, away at Harvard, and eleven-year-old Willie and eight-year-old Tad. Early in 1862 Willie developed a serious fever and died after a brief

MARY TODD LINCOLN

illness. His devastated father lamented, "My poor boy, he was too good for this earth. . . ." Mary Todd Lincoln became mentally unbalanced, consumed with grief for the remainder of the war.

Varina Howell Davis

VARINA HOWELL DAVIS

was equally devoted to her growing family when she moved into the Confederate White House in Richmond with her three children: Margaret; Jefferson, Jr.; and Joseph. As first lady, she kept her White House full of guests and maintained a full social schedule, even while pregnant. Such activity was not the custom for most Southern ladies, and her behavior scandalized Confederate society. In 1861 in Richmond, another son, William, was born; three years later she gave birth to another daughter, Varina. But in 1864 a terrible tragedy befell the Davis family when five-year-old Joseph, playing on a balcony at home, tumbled two stories to his death. President Davis and his wife were inconsolable, but they had to set aside their grief and continue with the terrible business of war.

ANTIETAM, SHARPSBURG, MARYLAND

I n the autumn of 1862, in the cornfields of Maryland, more Americans lost their lives on a single day of battle than ever before or since. The number of Americans who died near Antietam Creek was more than twice the number of dead in the War of 1812, the Mexican War, and the Spanish-American War combined.

Lincoln visited General McClellan to urge him to pursue Lee's army across the Potomac River.

A daring Robert E. Lee wanted to invade Maryland, carrying the war north of the Potomac River to obtain supplies and to buy time for Virginia to recover from the ravages of war. Perhaps a victory on Northern soil would bring France or England in on the side of the Confederacy. Lee counted on the typical caution of Union General George McClellan, but McClellan moved more quickly than Lee had hoped. When Lee arrived near Antietam Creek on September 15, the Confederate commander decided to fight at Antietam.

September 17 dawned gray and foggy, as Union artillery erupted. All day long, fighting continued in the cornfields and woods and along a sunken road that would soon earn the nickname "Bloody Lane." Union General Ambrose Burnside took most of the day to capture a bridge over the creek and by the time it was taken from the five hundred Georgia rifleman defending it, Confederate reinforcements arrived, saving Lee from disaster.

BATTLE AT-A-GLANCE

ANTIETAM
Sharpsburg, Maryland,
September 17

Union troops: 75,000
Confederate troops: 40,000

Union casualties: 12,400
Confederate casualties: 10,300
DRAW

The dead at Dunker Church, near Antietam.

Lincoln Spares a Soldier's Life

Early on the morning of August 31, 1861, while on guard duty, a young man who had recently enlisted with the Vermont Volunteers fell sound asleep. For sleeping on the job, Private William Scott was arrested, tried, and ordered to be hanged on September 9.

The men of Scott's regiment submitted a petition to Lincoln, begging that the young boy be pardoned. The president, known to have a soft heart, responded, "I do not think an honest, brave soldier, conscious of no crime but sleeping when he was weary, ought to be shot or hung. The country has better uses for him." Lincoln granted clemency, a legal pardon that forgave Scott and allowed him to return to duty.

Young Scott died seven months later in combat, and newspapers described his noble death. A poem about him, "The Sleeping Sentinel," was read before the U.S. Senate in January 1863.

McClellan forced Lee to abandon his invasion, but he could not claim a complete victory. Southern troops managed to slip back across the Potomac River to Virginia, and Lincoln relieved McClellan for his failure to pursue Lee.

Because he was looking for the right time to "strike at the heart of the rebellion," Lincoln decided to emphasize Lee's retreat and claim Antietam as a Union victory. The president believed that emancipating runaway slaves would strip Southern plantations of valuable labor and provide an important resource for the Union army. He would free only those slaves belonging to Rebel masters and not interfere with Union slave owners.

On September 22 Lincoln announced his plan for emancipating all the slaves in Rebel states. By declaring that all Southern slaves would be freed January 1, he signaled that the Union was moving closer to total war, threatening to crush the rebellion by any means necessary.

GRANT APPROACHES VICKSBURG

Vicksburg was a marvel. Perched high atop a bluff over the Mississippi River, virtually unapproachable from three sides and heavily fortified, the town was called the "Gibraltar of the West." This Confederate outpost commanded a view of the river for miles in both directions, so approaching ships and soldiers could be easily picked off.

In December Union General William T. Sherman slogged through a swampy bayou as he headed toward Vicksburg, but Confederates held him off. Although the Union also launched a vigorous naval assault, General Ulysses S. Grant knew that skill, cunning, and patience would be needed to defeat the Confederates, who looked down from their high perch at Vicksburg and jeered at Union failures. Another six months of starvation and deprivation, of attacks on land and sea, would pass before the town of Vicksburg would finally be forced to surrender.

Conscientious Objectors

In all wars, some people are morally opposed to killing, even to defend their country. During the Civil War, many religious groups opposed to war faced a moral dilemma. For example, although the Society of Friends, Quakers, were pacifists who spoke out against war, they were also opposed to slavery. The Quakers had founded the first antislavery societies in the American colonies. They were extremely active in the Underground Railroad and they wanted to help freed slaves with food, clothing, and education. Most Quakers supported the Union cause.

When they were drafted, people whose beliefs would not permit them to fight were allowed to serve in other than combat roles and were given the legal status of "conscientious objectors."

Forced to enlist against his will, Cyrus Pringle, a Quaker from Burlington, Vermont, described his experience: "They are utterly unable to comprehend the pure Christianity and spirituality of our principles. They have long stiffened their necks in their own strength. They have stopped their ears to the voice of the Spirit, and hardened their hearts to his influences. They see no duty higher than to country. What shall we receive at their hands?" Held in a guardhouse, Pringle appealed directly to President Lincoln, who responded that he could do nothing but give him hospital duty. Such work was the "alternate service" offered to most conscientious objectors.

MATHEW BRADY AND PHOTOGRAPHY

When all of Washington was astir over the First Battle of Bull Run, Mathew Brady was a studio photographer whose specialty was producing portraits of the rich and famous. At his popular studio in Washington, D.C., the manager was Alexander Gardner, a Scottish immigrant who was a pioneer of wet-plate photography. Brady knew there would be an explosion in the demand for portraits, because every soldier going off to fight wanted an image of himself in uniform to leave with family, sweethearts, and friends at home. Soldiers equally treasured a photographic souvenir of loved ones to take to camp. When the war erupted on the outskirts of the District of Columbia, Brady recalled, "My feet said 'Go' and I went."

Brady's traveling caravan included heavy photographic equipment. Less than a quarter century old, photography was a relatively new art form, and taking pictures outside a studio was a painstaking process. Heavy 8-by-10-inch-glass plates, stored in total darkness on the wagon, were loaded into bulky cameras for effective still shots in the field. Once the shutter was tripped, the plate had to be carefully treated and transported.

Though Brady, himself, took few photographs during the war, his employees recorded hundreds of views. These Civil War photographs provided visual records of the war, and also personalized the ordeal by showing the faces

A railroad bridge, one of many that the U.S. Army constructed quickly.

Mathew Brady (at right) with Union officers in their camp.

of soldiers and the grim details of battle. The photographs of Gettysburg remain especially haunting. Sometimes photographers even improved upon nature and rearranged corpses to create a more striking image.

Most battlefield shots credited to the near-blind Brady were taken by others, notably Alexander Gardner and Timothy O'Sullivan. Gardner eventually left Brady's employ, opened his own shop, and worked for the Union War Department. In 1866 he published his masterwork, *Photographic Sketch Book of the War,* which offered a vivid visual record of the war. The rise of wartime photography is forever associated with the name of Mathew Brady, whose fate was sealed when he followed his feet to the First Battle of Bull Run.

TECHNOLOGICAL ADVANCES

When the Civil War began, both the North and South thought they knew what to expect from battle. But the American Civil War witnessed accelerated improvement of weaponry that dramatically changed warfare.

Northerners were able to take advantage of their booming railroad industry. The U.S. Army assigned twenty-four thousand men to a railway construction and repair corps. For the first time ever, large numbers of soldiers were sent to the front by rail, sometimes in bulletproof cars. And portable, preassembled railway trusses, easy to transport and install, made the rebuilding of blown-up bridges much easier. The destroyed Chattahoochee Bridge, more than 800 feet long and 100 feet high, was restored to use in less than five days!

Over the course of the war, soldiers employed more and more efficient firepower. The muskets of 1861, which were loaded from the muzzle, or barrel, were by 1864 being replaced by breech-loading rifles, which could be much more quickly loaded from the back. Though most soldiers still fought with muzzle loaders, the cavalry soldiers carried lighter, shorter rifles called carbines, which were even easier to handle. The minié ball, an inch-long bullet, improved the average soldier's aim nearly 500 percent. Now soldiers could shoot at the enemy more quickly and accurately.

The Union also purchased Agar machine guns, which looked like coffee mills but could fire 120 minié balls a minute, and Vandenberg guns, which contained 85 to 450 barrels per gun, were mounted on a carriage, and were able to fire 65 rounds per minute. Yankee soldiers were supplied with the Gatling gun, invented in 1862, which had 6 barrels revolved by a crank and could fire very rapidly without reloading. But very few of these modern weapons ever saw use. Samuel Colt had invented the pistol in 1835, and during the war the Colt factory produced the favorite handgun for American soldiers. The grenade, a handheld bomb, also came into use, but these early grenades lacked a safety device.

Confederates had fewer gun factories and ammunition manufacturers to supply them with new improved weapons and bullets. Rebels were dependent on foreign sales, smuggled weapons, and guns collected from the enemy. In 1862 more than a hundred thousand Union rifles were "harvested" from battlefields by Confederates. Soldiers were desperate to take advantage of these great advances in technology, which ironically made war even more deadly.

Balloons at War

One of Lowe's observation balloons.

As head of the Balloon Corps, Thaddeus Lowe was in charge of the Union army's most pioneering weapon. Hydrogen balloons provided the great advantage of observing the enemy from above. Lowe's horse-drawn hydrogen generators often headed for the battlefield, along with one of his observation balloons, such as the *Intrepid.* Hundreds of ascensions (flights upward to observe) were made during McClellan's Virginia campaign in 1862 and into the spring of 1863. Lowe himself frequently went aloft. The balloon was tethered to the ground by rope, with a light telegraph wire attached so the man in the basket below the balloon could report on what he saw in the distance. Telescopes allowed the observer to "sketch the line," accurately assessing the strength and placement of the enemy during battle. This ability was so valuable that the Confederates, who had no balloon corps, felt themselves at a distinct disadvantage.

BATTLE OF FREDERICKSBURG
FREDERICKSBURG, VIRGINIA

Union General Ambrose Burnside, who had replaced George McClellan as head of the Army of the Potomac, knew he had to strike at the Confederate capital, Richmond, or he, too, would be fired. Burnside had a daring plan—to march his force of more than a hundred thousand across the Rappahannock River on bridges of floating structures called pontoons. He launched his operation near the small town of Fredericksburg, halfway between the two capitals, Richmond and Washington. Unfortunately, Lee had anticipated the Union attack and fortified his positions near the riverfront.

Confederate sharpshooters picked off many of the soldiers in blue as they crossed on pontoons. When they tried to storm up a steep hill called Marye's Heights, Burnside's men were mowed down. The slaughter was intense and awful, as charge after charge of Yankees was turned back. One Confederate commander described the bravery of the Union men, who "melt[ed] like snow coming down on warm ground." Indeed, snowflakes covered the ground where bodies didn't on the raw December day in Fredericksburg, where thousands of Union soldiers lay dead.

BATTLE OF STONES RIVER
MURFREESBORO, TENNESSEE

On the frozen western front, in the dead of winter, while most commanders on both sides had suspended fighting until spring, the overconfident Confederate General Braxton Bragg launched an attack on Union forces near Murfreesboro, Tennessee, where Union General William S. "Rosey" Rosecrans had set up winter quarters. All day long on December 31, fighting was bitter. Bragg, anticipating victory, telegraphed Richmond, "God has granted us a happy New Year." But when New Year's Day finally dawned, Rosecrans had held his position and fought off the Rebels. Bragg ordered another assault on January 2, but his officers insisted on retreating instead. Heavy casualties and his men's lack of support forced Bragg's withdrawal, making the Battle of Stones River a terrible loss of face for the Confederates.

EYEWITNESS

"Hard fighting does not begin to express the work that was done. I never want to see another engagement. 'To what did it amount?'. . .We can never whip the Rebels. I believe. Let those who talk of the valor of our troops—which is all true—come and see the Rebels fight. Why not settle the difficulty at once without further expense and loss of life? . . . Why not confess we are worsted, and come to some agreement? . . . Why murder your sons and brothers for no commensurate result?"

SAMUEL EDMUND NICHOLS,
a Union soldier writing in despair
to his cousin Phoebe, after the
Battle of Fredericksburg

Fredericksburg after the battle.

NEW YEAR'S RESOLUTIONS

When 1862 drew to a close, both North and South had suffered enormous loss of life and morale. Lincoln was reeling over the drastic losses at Fredericksburg. He was worried that the mounting death lists posted at general stores and at railway depots throughout the North would turn the country against the war, as well as against him as the president responsible for it.

Similarly, President Jefferson Davis had to deal with strong-willed generals like Braxton Bragg and other independent Confederate officers, who boasted that they would "whip the Yankees," but who sometimes ended up defeated.

Despite military setbacks, the Confederates had managed to hold on to the upper Mississippi River, which kept supplies flowing between the upper South and the Delta region. Jackson and Lee claimed important victories in Virginia, which lifted sagging Southern spirits. But during the autumn of 1862, Lincoln attempted to pull the rug out from under Rebel triumphs by promising to free the slaves. He knew his preliminary outline of plans for the Emancipation Proclamation in January 1863 would undermine Confederate campaigns to gain diplomatic recognition or further economic support abroad. In addition, his offer of freedom and refuge to millions of slaves trapped within Rebel borders would signal an important shift. Confederate leaders realized that Lincoln's new moral agenda, as well as the infusion of black soldiers into the Union army, might alter the course of the war and redefine the terms of peace.

BATTLES AT-A-GLANCE

BATTLE OF FREDERICKSBURG
Fredericksburg, Virginia, December 13

Union troops: 120,000
Confederate troops: 75,000

Union casualties: 12,500
Confederate casualties: 5,300
CONFEDERATE VICTORY

BATTLE OF STONES RIVER
Murfreesboro, Tennessee December 31–January 2

Union troops: 45,000
Confederate troops: 12,400

Union casualties: 38,000
Confederate casualties: 12,000
UNION VICTORY

Irish Brigade
IMMIGRANTS AND THE UNION ARMY

When the Civil War erupted, huge numbers of Irish immigrants in the United States enlisted. The fighting Irish marched into battle with sprigs of evergreen tucked in their caps at the Battle of Fredericksburg. By the time the sun set, only two hundred fifty of the fourteen hundred men in the brigade survived. This heroic immigrant company had followed its leader, Thomas Francis Meagher (right).

Meagher was born into a wealthy family in Ireland. His radical politics got him into trouble, and he emigrated to New York City in 1852. When the Civil War began, Meagher urged his fellow countrymen to join the Union army. His Irish volunteers fought in the First Battle of Bull Run.

Meagher then filled an entire brigade with Irish soldiers. The flamboyant recruiter wore a colorful uniform and was an eloquent speaker. He drew Irish volunteers from all over, but mostly from eastern cities crowded with immigrants.

Despite the Irish Brigade's losses at Antietam and Fredericksburg, the brave men remained fighting together under their regimental green silk flags.

CHAPTER 4

1863

As the second anniversary of the war neared, Lincoln electrified the nation by issuing the Emancipation Proclamation. This proclamation freed all the slaves in the South. Thousands of black refugees poured into Union camps seeking federal protection. By the summer of 1863, African-American men were entering Union military ranks in increasing numbers, and the divide between the two warring sides grew even wider.

In a bold gamble, Confederate General Robert E. Lee led his army deep into the North and engaged in a desperate clash near the small Pennsylvania town of Gettysburg. This encounter has been called "the hinge of fate" because during the battle the outcome of the entire war may have hung in the balance.

Union General Ulysses S. Grant's persistent campaign in Mississippi finally paid off and Rebel soldiers at Vicksburg wearily surrendered. Both Union victories were achieved on the country's birthday, Independence Day, July 4. Lee lost at Gettysburg and Grant triumphed at Vicksburg—more than a thousand miles apart.

President Lincoln, who hoped surrender would be near, worried as the Confederacy continued to pursue its decaying dream of independence, almost at any cost.

A flotilla of Union gunboats steaming up the Mississippi during the siege at Vicksburg.

THE YEAR AT-A-GLANCE

January 1
Emancipation Proclamation

May 1–5
Battle of Chancellorsville
Chancellorsville, Virginia

July 1–3
Battle of Gettysburg
Gettysburg, Pennsylvania

July 4
Surrender at Vicksburg
Vicksburg, Mississippi

September 19–20
Battle of Chickamauga
Chickamauga, Georgia

November 19
Lincoln's Gettysburg Address
Gettysburg, Pennsylvania

November 23–25
Battle of Chattanooga
Chattanooga, Tennessee

An Emancipation Proclamation poster, with Lincoln prominently featured below the text.

The fight to save the Union took on an important moral tone when Lincoln decided to free Southern slaves. The war might have begun over sectional differences and an effort to save the Union, but Lincoln's decision to destroy Southern slaveholding transformed the battle into a crusade for liberty, offering the promise of democratic ideals for all Americans.

Opponents accused Lincoln of having less than noble motives for emancipation. They pointed out that Lincoln did not abolish slavery for Union slaveholders in the border states. If he was acting solely as an opponent of slavery, why did he allow slaveholders in Union states to keep their slaves?

Whatever his intentions, Lincoln has become known as the "Great Emancipator." He set the wheels in motion for the majority of black Americans to escape the bonds of slavery and take their place alongside whites in the fight to preserve the Union.

Abolitionists cheered Lincoln's decision, which they felt would not only lead to acceptance of African Americans into the Union army, but might eventually lead to racial equality within the reunited country.

EYEWITNESS

"When the people saw me coming with the paper in my hand they raised a shouting cheer that was almost deafening. As many as could get around me lifted me to a great platform, and I started to read the proclamation. . . . Men squealed, women fainted, dogs barked, white and colored people shook hands, songs were sung, and by this time cannons began to fire at the navy yard. . . . Great processions of colored and white men marched to and fro in front of the White House and congratulated President Lincoln on his proclamation."

REVEREND HENRY M. TURNER,
African-American minister
Washington, D.C., January 1

UNITED STATES COLORED TROOPS

Frederick Douglass spoke often and eloquently about the right of his fellow black Americans to serve in the Union army. He condemned federal policy, which allowed the "white hand" to fight while telling the "black hand" to hold back. African-American leaders rejoiced when men of color took up arms. Douglass proclaimed, "Let the black man get upon his person the brass letters U.S., let him get an eagle on his button and a musket on his shoulder. There is no power on earth which can deny that he earned the right to citizenship in the United States." Both free blacks and fugitive slaves had wanted to fight since the beginning of the war. Finally, in 1863, the War Department authorized the recruitment and enlistment of African Americans into the Union army.

Despite Confederate resistance, federal forces drained plantations of slaves. One former mistress, angry at confronting her former slave in a Yankee uniform, reminded him that she had nursed him when he was sick, and "now you are fighting me!" The man

African-American soldier with his family.

African Americans celebrate the end of slavery in this image from a French newspaper.

calmly replied, "No'm, I ain't fighting you, I'm fighting to get free."

Black men had to fight racism in the Union ranks because many Yankee soldiers did not support emancipation. Kept in segregated units, black soldiers performed with courage, discipline, and pride under very difficult circumstances. One of the most famous of the black regiments, the 54th Massachusetts, was composed mainly of Northern free blacks. Two of Frederick Douglass's sons served with this regiment.

Not only black men, but also black women joined the war effort. Former slave Harriet Tubman, once a "conductor" on the Underground Railroad, became a scout for the Union army in South Carolina. She helped Union General David Hunter bring hundreds of runaways to safety behind Union lines during summer raids in 1863. Northern free black women, like Charlotte Forten of Philadelphia, came south to establish schools and missions to assist former slaves where Union troops were stationed in occupied South Carolina.

NO MORE AUCTION BLOCK

"No more auction block for me,
No more, no more,
No more auction block for me,
Many thousands gone.

No more peck of corn for me,
No more, no more,
No more peck of corn for me,
Many thousands gone.

No more pint of salt for me,
No more, no more,
No more pint of salt for me,
Many thousands gone.

No more driver's lash for me,
No more, no more,
No more driver's lash for me,
Many thousands gone."

SONG CELEBRATING
EMANCIPATION PROCLAMATION

Susie King Taylor

Susie King Taylor, the granddaughter of an African slave brought to Georgia during the 1730s, was born on a Georgia plantation in 1848. She went to live with her grandmother in Savannah, where she had white playmates willing to teach her to read and write. When the war broke out in 1861, Taylor recalled the horrid shelling of nearby Fort Pulaski: "I remember what a roar and din the guns made. They jarred the earth for miles."

When federals captured the fort, Taylor fled with her family to Hilton Head, South Carolina, a nearby island where Union officers were stationed.

The white officers there drafted her to teach freed slaves. She married a sergeant with the 1st South Carolina Volunteers and served alongside him as a nurse and laundress for the troops. She confided, "I learned to handle a musket very well while in the regiment, and could shoot straight and often hit the target." Taylor assisted Clara Barton in nursing the troops, when Barton moved in to work in the islands. Taylor remained with her husband's regiment until the Union troops liberated Charleston in February 1865. In 1902 she wrote *My Life in Camp With the 33rd United States Colored Troops, Late 1st S.C. Volunteers*, and she became the only African-American woman to publish a memoir of wartime service.

The constant cry for bread in the South echoed from the banks of the Shenandoah River in Virginia to the Mississippi delta as the need for food spread everywhere. Civilians and soldiers alike were desperate for supplies. Because white men had been at war for two planting seasons, harvests were poor and grain storehouses were nearly empty.

Southern housewives faced with bare pantries tried substitutions: raspberry leaves for tea leaves, okra seeds for coffee beans, cottonseed oil for kerosene. Many mistresses gathered herbs in the woods, "our drugstores," as one woman called them. Louisa McCord

The streets of the Confederate capital during the bread riot, as imagined by a Northern newspaper illustrator.

Smythe described conditions in Charleston: "Food was frightfully scarce and what there was was of the coarsest descriptions. . . ." An Atlanta storekeeper reported that a veteran's wife, toting a gun, simply took food for her starving family when she had no money to pay.

By the spring of 1863, the Confederate capital, Richmond, was crowded with hungry refugees. In early April, a band of a thousand women and children "marched silently and in order," emptying stores to feed their families and to protest the lack of food. Soldiers were called out to clear the streets, but the crowd of angry women refused to budge. Blaming the Confederate president for their shortages, they hissed when Jefferson Davis first appeared. He calmed the rioters by promising them rations of rice. Only after three days did the government regain control of the city.

EYEWITNESS

"*We are starving. As soon as enough of us get together we are going to the bakeries and each of us will take a loaf of bread. That is little enough for the government to give us after it has taken all our men.*"

ANONYMOUS WOMAN
in Richmond

"Captain" Sally Tompkins

Perhaps the most famous nurse in the Confederacy, Sally Tompkins worked side by side with her slaves. Confederate President Davis awarded Tompkins a military commission as captain, the only woman to receive such an honor.

Tompkins was born into a wealthy planter family and was living in Richmond when news of Fort Sumter arrived. Twenty-eight and unmarried, she threw herself wholeheartedly into the Confederate cause. In Richmond after the first major battle of the war at Bull Run, Tompkins reported, "It is now nearly 2 o'clock Sunday night—

but I am so excited by the news of our glorious victory that I cannot sleep. . . ."

Tompkins persuaded Judge John Robertson to allow his Richmond home to become a hospital for Confederate wounded. In her four years managing Robertson's Hospital, Tompkins treated more than twelve hundred sick and wounded, losing fewer than twenty patients. She has remained a heroine to Southerners for her dedicated service.

Military Medical Care

In both Union and Confederate armies, each regiment was assigned a doctor, called a surgeon, to provide medical care after battles. A yellow flag, 6 feet by 4 feet, marked field hospitals, the tents or buildings where surgeons performed operations. Soldiers with bright armbands carried the injured off the field on stretchers.

From crutches to scalpels, Civil War medical equipment was both scarce and valuable for army doctors.

The Confederate doctors were at a disadvantage because the simplest drugs often did not make it through the blockade. Operations and amputations sometimes had to be performed without giving the patient anything to deaden the pain.

Even under the best circumstances, the operating table was little more than a rubber sheet,

The most typical battle injury was a bullet wound. A soldier's chances of survival pretty much depended on where he was hit: Shots in the chest were almost always fatal. The poet Walt Whitman, a nurse during the war, described conditions in Washington where he served: "There is every kind of wound, in every part of the body. . . . There are twice as many sick as there are wounded. The deaths range from 7 to 10 percent of those under treatment." Infections posed a constant threat, and during the Civil War, for every soldier killed in battle, almost two died of disease.

Surgeons in the field, forced to make hard choices, did the best they could under primitive conditions.

rarely sponged clean between surgeries. Surgeons cleaned instruments by simply dipping them in pans of water. The absence of sterilized instruments and a general lack of cleanliness contributed to the spread of infection. It is no wonder that gangrene developed in one out of every five operations.

The Union, which had more and better hospitals than the South, provided better medical care. A few Southern facilities, such as Phoebe Pember's Chimborazo Hospital in Richmond, could match what the Yankees offered. Kate Cumming of Mobile, Alabama, reported that she had to kneel in blood to treat patients. A Confederate nurse named Sarah Rice Pryor remembered working grueling twelve-hour shifts after battles to save the wounded men.

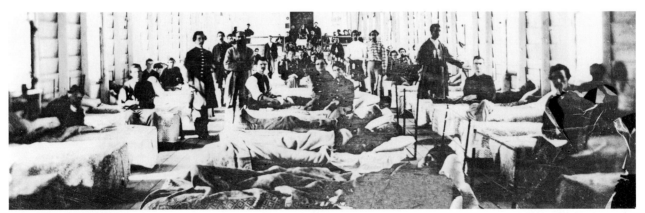

Men were crowded into wards in this Union military hospital. Women nurses had to remove their hoops to move through the aisles between the sickbeds.

After the bloody repulse at Fredericksburg, Union General Ambrose Burnside was relieved of his command. Lincoln replaced him with a more aggressive military leader, General Joseph "Fighting Joe" Hooker, who was eager to take charge. Hooker had a reputation for being concerned about his troops, so he began at once to improve morale. A soldier confided, "I have never known men to change from a condition of the lowest depression to that of a healthy fighting state in so short a time." But Hooker was also an astute politician and engineered his rise through the Union ranks by cultivating power.

Once spring arrived and the roads were less muddy, Hooker declared that he would pin Lee down at Chancellorsville and then send troops in from behind to finish him off. He believed his plan was foolproof, but Lincoln warned, "The hen is the wisest of all the animal creation because she never cackles until after the egg is laid."

With Hooker nearby, Confederate Generals Robert E. Lee and Stonewall Jackson decided to attempt the same daring military maneuver that the Union general had boasted he would accomplish—an ambush from the rear. Hooker's men were dug into the dense forested region known as "the Wilderness" to fight off Lee's advance. At this time, Jackson marched the bulk of the Confederate forces around to attack Hooker's troops from behind. This maneuver caught the Union completely by surprise and scattered the troops into the brambles. A Union witness recalled, "It was a whirlwind of men. The enemy seemed to come from every direction." As a result, the soldiers in blue were trapped and entangled and confused. Fires raged and men were caught in the dense burning woods.

An officer inspects Union artillery before the battle at Chancellorsville.

Near the end of the battle, Lee forced Hooker's troops into retreat despite being outnumbered two to one. This defeat, a stunning blow to the Union army, paved the way for Hooker to be relieved of his command the last week of June, after less than six months in charge. He was replaced by General George Meade.

The triumph of the Confederacy at Chancellorsville was bittersweet, however. A tragic accident occurred when General Jackson was accidentally wounded by his own men during the battle. General J.E.B. Stuart replaced this key commander when the fallen Jackson was carried off. A few days later, Lee and the Confederate nation mourned Jackson's death.

One of the most enduring Confederate images of the war, the *Last Meeting of Lee and Jackson*, (shown at left) was painted in 1869. Reproductions hung in many Southern homes as a tribute to these two great military leaders.

DEATH OF STONEWALL JACKSON

Beloved, eccentric General Thomas J. Jackson was at the peak of his military powers when he joined Lee near Chancellorsville. The two generals had spent the recent Christmas together, and Lee had attended the christening of Jackson's daughter weeks before. The two comrades met shortly before midnight on May 1 to plan strategy for the next day of battle. Lee believed that Jackson could pull off a miraculous maneuver and surprise the Union men from behind. Indeed, Jackson's men performed beautifully the next day.

But in the darkness and confusion of returning to camp, Jackson was hit by a bullet from one of his own men. As they carried him to safety, his officers had to make a human shield to protect his body from the gunfire. The doctor was forced to amputate Jackson's left arm. Hearing the news, Lee said: "He has lost his left arm, but I have lost my right."

At first Stonewall Jackson seemed on the road to recovery. But by the time his wife, Mary Anna, arrived, pneumonia had set in and he was fading. On the morning of Sunday, May 10, Jackson's doctor warned that he might die. Anna broke the news to her husband, a deeply religious man. Jackson replied, "I have always desired to die on Sunday." He became delirious, shouting orders as if he were still in the thick of battle. Finally he closed his eyes and spoke his dying words: "Let us cross over the river and rest under the shade of the trees."

When Jefferson Davis declared a day of national mourning, the Confederacy bowed its head. Stonewall Jackson was buried in Lexington, not far from the grounds of the Virginia Military Institute, a shattering loss to his family and his comrades.

Female mourners gathered at Jackson's grave near the Virginia Military Institute, where he once taught.

Jubilant after Chancellorsville, Confederate commanders pushed northward. Lee decided to cross the Potomac into Maryland and invade Pennsylvania. During the invasion, Southern soldiers went looking for food and supplies. Confederate Commander A. P. Hill sent his men off to find clothing and shoes rumored to be stored in the nearby town of Gettysburg. These soldiers stumbled onto Union forces, setting off a chain reaction. Some believe that what followed was the most decisive encounter between North and South in the entire war. Almost one out of every three soldiers in the battle was killed, wounded, or missing in action.

Early in the morning of July 1, both General Lee (unsure about the size of the force he faced) and Union General George Meade concentrated on getting their men into a good fighting position. Most of the men in both armies were still marching toward Gettysburg. The soldiers fought vigorously, moving along the Chambersburg Road, closer and closer to the center of Gettysburg.

More than 3,000 federal soldiers were captured on the first day. The Confederates lost 6,500 men and the Union an additional 6,000. Although Confederates had control of Gettysburg, commanders on both sides knew the fight was undecided and would continue the next day.

BATTLE AT-A-GLANCE

BATTLE OF GETTYSBURG
Gettysburg, Pennsylvania, July 1–3

Union troops: 85,000
Confederate troops: 75,000

Union casualties: 23,000
Confederate casualties: 28,000
UNION VICTORY

One of Mathew Brady's photographers captured this view of Little Round Top, the scene of fierce fighting. Brady, standing with his arm against a tree at left in the picture, surveys the scene.

POINT of VIEW

AT LITTLE ROUND TOP

NORTH

"The edge of the conflict swayed to and fro, with wild whirlpools and eddies. At times I saw around me more of the enemy than of my own men; gaps opening, swallowing, closing again; squads of stalwart men who had cut their way through us, disappearing as if translated. All around a strange, mingled roar. . . . An officer fired his pistol at my head with one hand, while he handed me his sword with the other. . . ."

COLONEL JOSHUA LAWRENCE CHAMBERLAIN,
Commander, 20th Maine Regiment

SOUTH

"I again ordered the advance . . . waving my sword, shouting, 'Forward men, to the ledge!' and was promptly followed by the command in splendid style. [The 20th Maine] charged my line, coming right up in a hand to hand encounter. . . .We ran like a herd of wild cattle. As we ran, a man . . . to my right and rear had his throat cut by a bullet. . . . My dead and wounded were then nearly as great in number as those still on duty. They literally covered the ground. . . ."

COLONEL WILLIAM C. OATES,
Commander, 15th Alabama Regiment

LITTLE ROUND TOP, JULY 2

On the second day of battle, the three Chamberlain brothers from Maine galloped toward a rise overlooking the battlefield that came to be known as Little Round Top. A federal officer had reported that Confederate troops had taken Big Round Top and sent for reinforcements to protect the Union position overlooking the entire battlefield. When a Confederate shell barely missed the Chamberlains riding alongside one another, Joshua, the colonel in command of the 20th Maine, sent one of his brothers to the rear and the other to the front to be his eyes and ears. What they saw was incredible, a force of Alabama Rebels twice their number! The three hundred fifty Maine men rapidly took cover on the south slope of Little Round Top.

Five times the Johnny Rebs (Southern soldiers) charged up the hill, and five times the Billy Yanks (Northern soldiers) held off their advance. An incredible forty thousand rounds of ammunition were fired on the slope in an hour and a half of intense combat. Chamberlain knew that the Union troops were running out of bullets. In desperation, he ordered his men to fix their bayonets on the end of their rifles and led a brave charge down the hill. His courage saved the day, because the Alabama troops retreated and the Union held this valuable stronghold. Although Little Round Top was only a small part of the battle, it proved a crucial and symbolic encounter. Chamberlain was later awarded the Congressional Medal of Honor for his valor during this key battle.

General Lee attacked all along the Union line, but the Yankees managed to hold on. By the end of the second day of combat, the fields were littered with more than thirty-five thousand casualties, and both sides refused to retreat. A midnight council of Union commanders ended with Meade's prediction that Lee would attack front and center early the next day.

Men sometimes sent home sketches with their letters to better reveal the harsh nature of life at the front. Too many times these letters were the last communications between soldiers and their loved ones—especially after bloodbaths like Gettysburg.

PICKETT'S CHARGE, JULY 3

The wall of gray seemed to appear from nowhere on the third day of battle at Gettysburg. The Union soldiers saw the Rebels in formation half a mile wide. The federal soldiers held their fire, and perhaps even their breath, at the spectacle of nine Confederate brigades marching proudly forward.

Confederate General James Longstreet had advised a march around the Yankee army, but Lee insisted upon one last attempt to break through the federal line. The Union front stretched several miles—from a southern flank at Little Round Top, along a stretch called Cemetery Ridge, and northeastward, to Culp's Hill. Although General Longstreet was in command of this most famous Confederate assault, it became known as Pickett's Charge.

George Pickett and two other generals led their divisions to the attack. Despite Southern bravery, despite the pride and precision with which the men marched, the Confederates were slaughtered. More than fifty-six hundred men perished during this charge. The bloodbath washed away Confederate dreams, even as stories of Southern military glory spread. General Lewis Armistead had crossed over a stone wall into the Yankee lines with his hat on his sword, only to be fatally wounded moments later.

GENERAL GEORGE PICKETT

The majority of the Rebel casualties were mowed down even before they reached the Union line. All three divisions lost heavily. Pickett's division was cut to ribbons: Two-thirds of his men perished, and all thirteen of his colonels were killed or wounded. When Lee asked Pickett to prepare his division to fight off a counterattack, he replied: "General Lee, I have no division now."

The Confederates retreated southward to try to recover. Lee was so depressed that he offered his resignation to President Davis, maintaining that "a younger and abler man than myself can readily be obtained." Davis refused the offer, and Lee soldiered on.

After the war, Pickett's Charge remained perhaps the most powerful symbol of Confederate bravery, of courage in the face of death. Only some of the Southern soldiers who watched the blood of comrades being washed away during their retreat in the rain on July 4 realized that Gettysburg was the beginning of the end of the war. But most were determined to keep fighting. This battle has been characterized as the supreme moment of sacrifice for soldiers on both sides. The Confederacy lost 28,000 men (killed, wounded, captured, or missing), while the Union lost 23,000 at this little Pennsylvania crossroads called Gettysburg.

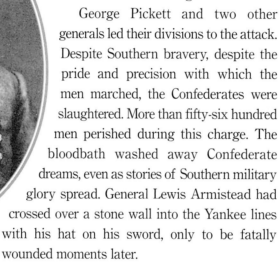

POINT OF VIEW

NORTH

"Valuable as New Orleans will be to us, Vicksburg will be even more so. We may take all the northern ports of the Confederacy, and they can still defy us from Vicksburg. It means hog and hominy without limit, fresh troops from all the states of the far South, and a cotton country where they can raise the staple without interference."

ABRAHAM LINCOLN

SOUTH

"Vicksburg . . . the nailhead that held the South's two halves together."

JEFFERSON DAVIS

EYEWITNESS

"*On returning [to the cave], an explosion sounded near her—one wild scream and she ran into her mother's presence, sinking like a wounded dove, the life blood flowing over the light summer dress in crimson ripples from a death wound in her side caused by the shell fragment.*"

MARY ANN LOUGHBOROUGH, recalling "cave life" in Vicksburg

The Fall of Vicksburg

Union troops take possession of Vicksburg.

By land and water, Union troops struggled toward Vicksburg, as they had since the summer of 1862. This port overlooking the Mississippi was the key to controlling the river and maintaining Confederate supply lines. Soldiers encountered every kind of obstacle, from polluted water ("With every pint of fluid one has to drink a half ounce of dirt") to insects ("Every soldier was a walking chigger cemetery") to dysentery, an inflammation of the bowels that the men nicknamed the "Mississippi quickstep."

In a desperate push, Union soldiers seized nearby Port Gibson, where sixteen thousand Rebel troops had previously menaced Union gunboats. For the Rebel soldiers trapped at Vicksburg, morale was even lower. A soldier's rations were limited to one biscuit a day and a little bacon. Federal soldiers joked that the Rebels were waiting for the arrival of a new general—"General Starvation."

On July 3 the Confederate commander finally sent a messenger with a flag of truce. Vicksburg surrendered and Grant claimed his prize on July 4. The news from Gettysburg reinforced Union hopes of victory, as a Southern general glumly observed: "The Confederacy totters to its destruction."

Union troops take possession of Vicksburg.

BATTLE AT-A-GLANCE

BATTLE OF VICKSBURG
Vicksburg, Mississippi, May 22
Surrender, July 4

Union troops: 77,000
Confederate troops: 29,500

Union casualties: 3,200
Confederate casualties: 500
UNION VICTORY

NEW YORK DRAFT RIOTS

On July 12, fire bells rang out in the night as buildings caught fire and terror reigned in New York City. It wasn't Confederate soldiers causing the alarm, but looters rioting over the federal government's policy of drafting soldiers.

As early as August 1862, state quotas, or required numbers, for soldiers were not being filled. Some Northern papers published "cowards' lists" to shame men into enlisting. In March 1863, Congress passed a Conscription Act requiring all men between the ages of twenty and forty-five to register for the draft. Feelings against the draft ran so high that a riot broke out after names were drawn by lottery in New York City.

Mobs roamed the city, burning draft offices, smashing windows, even looting Brooks Brothers, a men's clothing store for wealthy shoppers, to protest the fact that wealthy men were able to buy their way out of the military. If a rich man did not want to serve, he could pay a "substitute," someone to take his place. Some men were given "exemptions"—a legal excuse for not fighting, such as a physical disability like blindness.

The violence continued for three days. The angry mob of mostly working-class and immigrant whites, who blamed the war on the slaves, rather than on the slave owners, directed their rage at black citizens. Black churches and boardinghouses were attacked. A black orphanage was burned to the ground. Local police were unable to restore order, and federal troops were sent from Gettysburg to help. Calm finally returned, but only after forty army regiments ringed the city to restore order. More than a hundred had died and hundreds more were injured in this awful episode.

FORT WAGNER, SOUTH CAROLINA

Colonel Robert Gould Shaw, the son of wealthy Boston abolitionists, had volunteered and served in battle. After Lincoln issued his Emancipation Proclamation, Shaw offered to command the 54th Massachusetts, a regiment of African-American soldiers, drawn mainly from the free black communities of New England, New York, and Pennsylvania.

Shaw and his men finally got their chance for glory when they volunteered to head the assault on Fort Wagner on July 18. This fort was on the Atlantic Ocean just southeast of Charleston, South Carolina. Many feared that trying to capture the Confederate stronghold was hopeless, that thousands would die

COLONEL ROBERT SHAW

EYEWITNESS

"On the afternoon of July [13] a rabble attacked our house, breaking windowpanes, smashing shutters and partially demolishing the front door. . . . Just after midnight a second mob was gathering. As one of the rioters attempted to ascend the front steps, Father advanced into the doorway and fired point-blank into the crowd. The mob retreated and no further demonstration was made that night. The next day a third and successful attempt at entrance was effected. This sent Father over the back fence while Mother took refuge on the premises of a neighbor. . . . Under cover of darkness the police conveyed our parents to the Williamsburg ferry."

MARITCHA LYONS,
a fifteen-year-old
African American during the
New York Draft Riots

The initial attack on Fort Wagner, South Carolina, by Union soldiers was a military defeat, but an important moral victory for African-American soldiers, who proved themselves valiant in battle.

in the effort. Still, the 54th was willing to lead the charge. The fighting was fierce as the African-American soldiers bravely tried to scale the walls of the fort. When the order was given to retreat, Sergeant William Carney, a black soldier from New Bedford, Massachusetts, seized the colors from the fallen bearer, and despite several wounds, dragged the regimental flag back to safety. Carney was nominated for the Congressional Medal of Honor and was the first black to receive the award. The bravery of the 54th Massachusetts was exceptional, because the men lost nearly half their comrades, and suffered the death of Colonel Shaw. In 1897 a bronze memorial was unveiled on Boston Common to honor the heroic sacrifice of Shaw and his men.

Port Hudson Campaign

The surrender of Port Hudson, 250 miles south of Vicksburg, on July 9 was a devastating blow to the Confederates. The capture of the garrison meant the South's final fortress on the Mississippi was gone. As soldiers in gray marched away, they passed a message defiantly carved into a tree: "Beware Yankees! This road leads to hell!"

In an even greater blow to the Confederates, black soldiers were among the Union troops. The victory at Port Hudson confirmed that using blacks in combat would give advantage to the North. Blacks performed nobly, and they added nearly two hundred thousand soldiers to Union rosters.

General Nathaniel Banks, Union Commander at the siege of Port Hudson declared: "Their conduct was heroic! No troops could be more determined or more daring. They made, during the day, three charges upon the batteries of the enemy, suffering very heavy losses and holding their position at nightfall with the other troops on the right of our line. . . ."

BATTLE OF CHICKAMAUGA

Confederate General Braxton Bragg wanted to drive federal forces out of Chattanooga, Tennessee. The rival armies gathered on opposing sides of a creek in northern Georgia called Chickamauga, 12 miles south of Chattanooga. When Confederates advanced across the creek, they hoped to smash through federal positions and move on to Chattanooga. On the second day of the battle, most of the Union army was driven off the field in retreat, including the federal commander, General Rosencrans. But despite repeated attacks, Union General George Thomas kept his men steadfast and held his position on a hill. Thomas was a Virginian by birth who stayed loyal to the Union in the face of secession. His loyalty was repaid by his men's devotion, and he earned the nickname, the "Rock of Chickamauga."

After winning the battle, Bragg decided not to capture Chattanooga, appalling his fellow generals, Nathan Bedford Forrest and James Longstreet. The Confederate command squabbled, but Bragg prevailed, feeling that Confederate losses of more than eighteen thousand were already too high. A witness claimed the creek ran red with human blood, and ten Confederate generals had been killed or wounded. Although Union soldiers were encircled by the Southern army, Chattanooga remained firmly in federal hands.

DEDICATION AT GETTYSBURG

Four months after the battle, visiting journalists reported that the earth at Gettysburg remained blood-soaked in places. In November, six thousand people descended on the little town to pay their respects at the dedication of a Union cemetery. On the train ride through the Pennsylvania countryside, President Lincoln was distracted, brooding because his wife, Mary, had begged him to stay behind with their son Tad, ill with a fever. The couple were still mourning the death of another son, Willie, who had not survived a fever the year before.

Despite his private concerns, President Lincoln came to Gettysburg as the spiritual and political leader of his people. He knew it was important to give his war-torn country hope, as days of grief stretched into years of mourning.

The aftermath in Gettysburg had been horrible. The dead and wounded left behind outnumbered the living ten to one, and the shell-shocked citizens of Gettysburg heroically tried to identify and bury dead soldiers. Lincoln had to set aside personal concerns and help the nation come to grips with such tragedy.

The President had prepared brief but poetic remarks, which became known as the "Gettysburg Address." Before he spoke, he was relieved to receive a telegram informing him that his son had recovered.

Lincoln was only one of many speakers at the dedication ceremonies. His two-minute talk followed a two-hour oration by the featured speaker, former governor of Massachusetts Edward Everett. Though his brief remarks were not even reported by some attending journalists, today Lincoln's words are celebrated as one of the most eloquent meditations on war ever offered.

BATTLE AT-A-GLANCE

BATTLE OF CHICKAMAUGA
Chickamauga, Georgia
September 19–20

Union troops: 58,000
Confederate troops: 66,000

Union casualties: 16,200
Confederate casualties: 18,500
CONFEDERATE VICTORY

Johnnie Clem

Nine-year-old Johnnie Clem, along with his younger brother, ran away from home in Newark, Ohio. Clem joined the Union army to become a drummer boy.

He was with a Michigan regiment, the 22nd, at the Battle of Chickamauga. On the second day of fighting, Clem picked up a gun from one of his dying comrades. A Confederate officer on horseback demanded his surrender. When the Rebel officer raised his saber to strike, young Clem shot him off his horse. For his valor, Clem was promoted to the rank of sergeant. Headlines celebrated the "Drummer Boy of Chickamauga." Happy in the military life, Clem remained in the army until his retirement in 1916 as a general.

The Gettysburg Address

"Four score and seven years ago our fathers brought forth on this continent, a new nation, conceived in liberty and dedicated to the proposition that all men are created equal.

Now we are engaged in a great civil war, testing whether that nation or any nation so conceived and so dedicated can long endure. We are met on a great battlefield of that war. We have come to dedicate a portion of that field as a final resting place for those who here gave their lives that that nation might live. It is altogether fitting and proper that we should do this.

But in a larger sense, we can not dedicate—we can not consecrate—we can not hallow—this ground. The brave men, living and dead, who struggled here, have consecrated it, far above our poor power to add or detract. The world will little note nor long remember what we say here, but it can never forget what they did here. It is for us the living, rather, to be dedicated here to the unfinished work which they who fought here have thus far so nobly advanced. It is rather for us to be here dedicated to the great task remaining before us—that from these honored dead we take increased devotion to that cause for which they gave the last full measure of devotion—that we here highly resolve that these dead shall not have died in vain—that this nation, under God, shall have a new birth of freedom—and that government of the people, by the people, for the people, shall not perish from the earth."

Thousands crowded into the village of Gettysburg to honor the fallen federal soldiers with an emotional ceremony that exalted Union sacrifice. Prayers and speeches, especially Lincoln's touching address, comforted the widows and orphans in the audience.

BATTLE OF CHATTANOOGA

Squabbling among the western Confederate command was notorious. President Davis was forced to visit Braxton Bragg and his fellow generals to urge them to work together peacefully, but his advice seemed to fall on deaf ears. The generals continued to fight among themselves as they faced federal troops determined to maintain control of Chattanooga.

Lincoln sent Generals William T. Sherman and Joseph Hooker to assist in capturing key Tennessee positions and to open supply lines to Chickamauga, which was defended by General George Thomas. Sherman proved a fearless leader during the battle.

On November 24, Hooker's troops attacked the Rebel stronghold on Lookout Mountain. The Union attacks were stalling on the flanks, or along the ends of the enemy lines; but George Thomas's men broke through the center of the Rebel position, smashing the Confederate line along Missionary Ridge. The Confederate circle around Chattanooga was finally broken, and the city remained in Union hands.

Confederate hopes melted away with General Bragg's troops, who retreated southward into northern Georgia. After this spectacular triumph Lincoln gave Ulysses S. Grant the prize he had earned, command of all the Union armies. General Sherman was offered command of the western forces. The Union leaders now decided that instead of simply engaging the Confederate army in battle, Union forces would have to strike hard into the deep South and bring the civilian population to the point of surrender.

General Joseph Hooker poses with his staff. This confident warrior who was known as "Fighting Joe" once told his troops before going into battle, "May God have mercy on General Lee, for I will have none."

BATTLE AT-A-GLANCE

BATTLE OF CHATTANOOGA
Chattanooga, Tennessee,
November 23–25

Union troops: 56,000
Confederate troops: 46,000

Union casualties: 5,800
Confederate casualties: 6,700
UNION VICTORY

New Year's Resolutions

As 1864 approached, the Union commanders hoped they had finally demolished Confederate dreams of victory. They figured the Rebels would have to surrender eventually. The federal government's desperate campaign to control the Mississippi River in the West had finally been won, and the equally ferocious battle to control western Tennessee had paid off as well. The Union was pleased by its mounting military success.

Lincoln was thrilled with the Union victories and with his reliable new leader of all the armies, Ulysses S. Grant. At the same time, the Union president was concerned about the staggering loss of life on both sides and about the sacrifices the new year would demand from civilians.

Jefferson Davis urged his people to hang on. He hoped the Yankees would tire of war and maybe vote Lincoln out of office in the upcoming elections. Despite the military setbacks of the past year, Davis still believed that his forces were superior and that the South's defensive position remained an advantage. Though he hoped that military triumphs would renew the flagging spirits of his people, Lincoln also knew that a long road still lay ahead—both to crush the Confederacy and to end the war.

Native Americans and the Civil War

Native Americans from many nations enlisted during the Civil War. An estimated three thousand joined the Union army—Ely Parker, a Seneca, was a colonel on General Grant's staff—but the overwhelming majority sided with the Confederacy.

Most Cherokee lived in the South, and many were slave owners. Thousands of Cherokee joined the Confederate army, and one, Stand Waitie, even rose to the rank of general—the highest ranking Indian on either side. In all, nearly twelve thousand Native Americans served in the Confederate army, both in the ranks of the eleven all-Indian regiments and in integrated units from North Carolina, Tennessee, and Kentucky.

Sometimes Native American soldiers decorated their uniforms with traditional ornaments of silver or wore feathered headbands. One observer described, "Their dress was chiefly Indian costume—buckskin hunting shirts, dyed almost every color, leggings, and moccasins of the same material, with little bells, rattles, ear-rings, and similar paraphernalia. Many of

CONFEDERATE GENERAL STAND WAITIE

them were bareheaded and about half carried only bows and arrows, tomahawks, and war clubs."

Many other Native Americans, who tried to remain neutral, were dragged into military conflicts. In January 1864, Union Colonel Kit Carson trapped a group of Navajo in Canyon de Chelly in the New Mexico Territory. Under U.S. Army orders, Carson forced the Native Americans to trek to a fort nearly 300 miles away. This ordeal has become known among the Navajo as the "Long Walk."

American Indians in Wisconsin, joining the Union army.

CHAPTER 5

1864

By the third anniversary of the war, Lincoln finally had found generals worthy of his dreams of victory. On the other hand, Jefferson Davis had lost some of his best military men, along with much of the South's territory. But still the Confederacy fought on. As a result, the Union leaders decided to launch a different kind of warfare, a strategy they called "total war."

Lincoln was willing to use "total warfare"—designed to break the will of the people as well as defeat the Confederate army—to end the war quickly. The president encouraged his Union generals to gather supplies from the Southern countryside and then to burn and destroy farms in an effort to starve the Rebels out. The federal government hoped this ruthless policy would save the lives of Union soldiers.

General Ulysses S. Grant, in charge of all the Union armies, would coordinate efforts to crush the enemy. As Jefferson Davis tried to boost Southern morale, he faced terrible and mounting problems. Numbers in the Confederate army steadily dwindled, and increasing shortages made life in the South more and more difficult.

THE YEAR AT-A-GLANCE

April–May
Red River Campaign
Red River, Texas

May 5–6
Battle of the Wilderness
Wilderness, Virginia

June 3
Battle of Cold Harbor
Cold Harbor, Virginia

September 4
Fall of Atlanta
Atlanta, Georgia

November 8
Lincoln's Reelection

November 29
Sand Creek Massacre
Sand Creek, Colorado

November 16–December 22
Sherman's March to the Sea
Atlanta to Savannah, Georgia

December 15–16
Battle of Nashville
Nashville, Tennessee

December 22
Surrender of Savannah, Georgia

Union soldiers plotted strategy and lounged on church pews that had been carried outside near Spotsylvania, Virginia. General Grant leans over two seated men to study a map.

RED RIVER CAMPAIGN

Union military leaders in the West decided to send a show of force, an expedition along the Red River moving through Louisiana and into Texas, perhaps all the way to the Rio Grande. Led by Union General Nathaniel Banks, a force of nearly thirty thousand marched deep into Confederate territory.

The Texas border had seen very little fighting, and only eight thousand Rebel soldiers protected the region. The Confederates tried to stop the Union invasion at the little town of Mansfield on April 8. The Rebels captured twenty cannon and two hundred wagons from General Banks, but the next day, Banks counterattacked and drove the enemy from the battlefield.

During the retreat, Union gunboats along the Red River were nearly stranded when water levels dropped. Admiral David Porter was able to save his fleet when his men constructed a dam to allow the ships to escape. This Union invasion accomplished little and drained men and resources. It was one of the last independent campaigns in the West, because Grant ordered Union commanders to get his approval for all future military operations.

EYEWITNESS

"Using my musket for a crutch, I began to pull away the burning brushwood, and got some of them out. One of the wounded Johnnies . . . began to help. . . . We were trying to rescue a young fellow in gray. The fire was all around him. The last I saw of that fellow was his face. . . . His eyes were big and blue and his hair like raw silk surrounded by a wreath of fire. I heard him scream, 'O, Mother! O, God!' It left me trembling all over like a leaf. After it was over my hands were blistered and burned so I could not open and shut them; but me and them Rebs tried to shake hands."

ANONYMOUS UNION SOLDIER, during Wilderness campaign

Combat in the woods could be even more treacherous than fighting across an open field, as soldiers discovered in the Battle of the Wilderness.

BATTLE OF THE WILDERNESS

Smoke filled the Virginia woods on May 5, as troops began to stumble onto one another shortly after the fighting began. Grant had planned to try to lure Lee into open country, but Lee attacked Grant's men when they were still in the thick woods near Chancellorsville, Virginia, known as "the Wilderness."

The battle proved especially gruesome for soldiers, who stumbled on bodies and debris from fighting that had occurred in the very same woods the year before. Men described combat as blind and vicious, grappling at almost point-blank range. Both sides pushed hard and gained nothing after a fierce day of fighting. Grant ordered another attack for five o'clock the next morning, and for a while it looked like the federals would win. General James Longstreet, leading a counterattack for the Confederates, was seriously wounded by a volley

GENERAL NATHANIEL BANKS

mistakenly fired by his own troops. After two days of battle, the Union had lost nearly eighteen thousand men and not gained a foot.

During the night, fires raged in the forest, as troops tried to rescue the Union and Confederate wounded. But scores of injured soldiers were trapped by the flames and died in the woods. These ghastly losses did not stop the Union advance toward Richmond, however, because Grant insisted that his army press on. He headed southeast for Spotsylvania, Virginia, hoping to block the path between Lee and the Confederate capital.

BATTLE OF SPOTSYLVANIA

The Confederate soldiers were out of breath by the time they reached Spotsylvania Court House in their retreat from the Wilderness with Union troops on their heels. They barely had time to start building defenses because in less than an hour Union troops arrived and fighting broke out. The battle raged for five days.

Early on May 12, twenty thousand Yankees launched an all-out assault on the entrenched Confederates. The troops clashed violently again and again at a point known as the "Bloody Angle." As casualties mounted, bodies were stacked in the trenches. An oak tree crashed to the ground in mid-battle because its trunk had been cut in two by the constant gunfire. General Grant claimed, "The world has never seen so bloody and protracted a battle as the one being fought." The battle continued, and the Rebels were able to hold the Yankees until May 20, when the armies again marched southward. This overwhelming assault on the Confederates took a terrible toll.

Meanwhile, near Richmond, the South suffered another tremendous setback. The brilliant, thirty-one-year-old Confederate cavalry commander, J.E.B. Stuart, was mortally wounded on May 11 as he tried to block the Union cavalry riding toward Richmond. Grant was determined to press on. He promised Lincoln: "I propose to fight it out on this line if it takes all summer." But it took much longer than the summer.

Telegraph wires, as seen in this photograph, were crucial lines of communication between headquarters and the outside world. Commanders needed to be kept informed about progress and setbacks at the front.

BATTLES AT-A-GLANCE

RED RIVER CAMPAIGN
Red River, Texas
March 10–May 22

Union troops: 30,000
Confederate troops: 13,000

Union casualties: 1,300
Confederate casualties: 1,600
DRAW

BATTLE OF THE WILDERNESS
Wilderness, Virginia, May 5–6

Union troops: 115,000
Confederate troops: 60,000

Union casualties: 18,000
Confederate casualties: 7,500
DRAW

BATTLE OF SPOTSYLVANIA
Spotsylvania, Virginia, May 8–20

Union troops: 110,000
Confederate troops: 50,000

Union casualties: 17,000
Confederate casualties: 8,000
UNION VICTORY

The battlefield at Cold Harbor.

Throughout May, skirmishes between Confederate and Union armies in Virginia continued as they moved toward Richmond. Each side hoped for a good opportunity to win a major victory. By June 1, both sides were stalled near the crossroads of Cold Harbor, a short distance from the Confederate capital.

For three days Grant attacked, pounding away at Confederate positions. On June 3, a Union observer reported a combat ritual: "I noticed that many of the soldiers had taken off their coats and seemed to be engaged in sewing up rents in them. On closer examination it was found that the men were calmly writing their names and addresses on slips of paper and pinning them on the backs of their coats, so that their dead bodies might be recognized and their fate made known to their families at home."

In fact, seven thousand of those Union soldiers were killed or wounded in the first half hour of the June 3 charge at Cold Harbor. A tense standoff followed, because neither side was willing to retreat. Indeed, not until four days later were stretcher parties sent to rescue the wounded. Hundreds lay hurt and dying. Grant finally requested a truce, usually a sign of defeat, before both sides again moved on to more battles.

EYEWITNESS

"*I thought of home far away. . . . I wondered if my fate would ever be known to them. I had a horror of dying alone. . . . I was afraid that none of my regiment would ever find me, and that with the unknown dead who lay scattered around me I would be buried in one common ground. The thought was terrible. How I longed for day. Just that some one would see me die.*"

Confederate private
E. D. PATTERSON as he lay
wounded on the battlefield

At Cold Harbor, war correspondent Alfred Waud sketched Union soldiers breaking through enemy lines and taking prisoners.

BATTLE AT-A-GLANCE

BATTLE OF COLD HARBOR
Cold Harbor, Virginia, June 3

Union troops: 109,000
Confederate troops: 59,000

Union casualties: 12,000
Confederate casualties: 1,500
CONFEDERATE VICTORY

Trench Warfare

During the battles of 1864, the Confederates increasingly resorted to building embankments and digging trenches to place a protective shield around themselves and ward off Yankee attackers. The Union troops also dug in. From 1862 onward, both Washington, D.C., and Richmond were surrounded by rings of fortifications. The use of trenches to hold off attackers was a major departure for wartime strategy, and one that proved especially effective for the outnumbered and outgunned Rebel army.

Robert E. Lee took advantage of the extensive network of trenches that encircled Petersburg, Virginia—the city that held the key to Richmond to its north—and this strategy held back the enemy for nine months. Unable to capture the Rebel earthworks, Grant's army also constructed trenches and forts. In addition to the maze of trenches, Confederates dotted their defenses with military contraptions imported from France called *chevaux-de-frises*—sets of pointed stakes driven into a log. In effect, these devices created a spiked protective shield set in front of the trench. This added protection made the defenses better able to withstand direct assaults. During World War I, the *chevaux-de-frises* were replaced by barbed wire.

In addition, V-shaped trenches allowed the dug-in soldiers to create a "killing zone," a region where fire could be trained on the enemy from more than one direction. Enemy troops marched into the V and were fired upon from both right and left. This defensive technique proved extremely effective and was not tied exclusively to the terrain. In previous encounters whoever reached high ground first might have the advantage, but now soldiers could create their own terrain with trenches and embankments. The introduction of "zones" was another innovation of modern combat, which along with trench warfare proved useful to defensive positions and deadly to the attacking enemy.

During torrential rains, men might be up to their thighs in water and forced to sleep and eat in uncomfortable dugouts such as these Confederate trenches at Petersburg. The sharpened wooden stakes seen at the upper right would discourage Union troops from charging.

Grant left Cold Harbor, Virginia, and in a bold new strategy headed for Petersburg, 20 miles south of Richmond. He knew that if he could capture Petersburg he could halt rail traffic and starve out Richmond. Confederate General P.G.T. Beauregard, who had only 2,200 men, was well outnumbered by Grant's 75,000 troops.

However, the Union army delayed its attack long enough for Lee to send reinforcements; when the Yankees charged, they were slaughtered. In the first three days of battle, the Confederates were able to inflict a staggering 12,000 federal casualties.

The siege continued for weeks and months, with varying intensity and fighting as Grant tried time and again to break into the defenses. The armies had to battle not only each other, but the natural elements as well. First there was a six-week heat wave and drought. Men were parched and dry, and when rain finally came, they welcomed it. But then the deluge continued and soldiers were forced to stand guard duty in trenches waist-deep in water. Despite these horrible conditions, the siege lasted for nearly nine months. Petersburg did not fall until the end of the war.

BATTLE AT-A-GLANCE

SIEGE OF PETERSBURG
Petersburg, Virginia,
June 15, 1864–April 3, 1865

Union casualties: 42,000
Confederate casualties: 28,000
UNION VICTORY

Winslow Homer's famous painting *Defiance: Inviting a Shot Before Petersburg, Virginia, 1864* **captures the tense and desperate mood of the soldiers during their long siege.**

Union supply wagons rolled out of Petersburg after federal troops had conquered the city.

DISASTER AT THE CRATER, JULY 30

Union commanders decided to try new tactics to capture Petersburg. Several Union soldiers, former coal miners with the 48th Pennsylvania, suggested that the Confederate line could be broken by running a mine shaft under it. Their commander supervised the digging of a tunnel 510 feet long and 20 feet deep. The T-shaped tunnel extended as far as the Confederate line, where shafts reached 35 feet in either direction. The Union men planted four tons of gunpowder in the shafts and planned a surprise attack. Before dawn on July 30, the mine exploded, creating a 500-foot gap in the Confederate line and a hole that looked as though a giant had just scooped it out with his hands.

However, the Union troops were unable to break through as planned because they could not easily make a path through the rubble. Union forces—nearly fifteen thousand men—mistakenly began to pour into the crater as Confederates organized their lines around this Union-made hole and fired down on the men in blue who were trapped within. Union soldiers were shot like fish in a barrel, and there were nearly four thousand casualties. Grant declared this terrible and avoidable massacre a "stupendous failure."

African-American troops dashed into the Crater following the Union's misguided attempts to blast a hole through Confederate battlements surrounding Petersburg.

OPINION AT HOME

From the first encounter at Fort Sumter until the end of the war, the Union and Confederate governments fought a war of words, as well as battles. All Americans were affected by the conflict, and people from diverse groups and different parts of the country voiced opinions about the war.

"As we have received the grace of God in Christ, by the gospel, and are called to follow peace with all men, we cannot, consistent with our faith and conscience, bear the arms of war for the purposes of shedding the blood of any or do anything to justify or encourage it in others."
A delegation of Shakers, a religious sect, speaking in Washington, D.C.

"I told General Hunter we would gladly fight if our homes and firesides could be protected—that we would fight with white soldiers and go wherever wanted . . . . we are willing to put in our mite and share the same fate with the pale faces. . . ."
Chief Y-O-To-Wah, representing the Kansas tribes (Wea, Peoria, Miami and Piankashaw), at Leavenworth, Kansas, January 1862

"Come where we may all smoke the pipe of peace and friendship around our great council fire. Let all the civilized nations acquiesce in allegiance to the Confederacy."
John Ross, Cherokee chief, writing to Chief Opotheleyoholo of the Creek, August 1861

"Stand by the flag! Whether native or foreign born, Christian or Israelite, stand by it and you are doing your duty, and acting well your part on the side of liberty and justice."
THE JEWISH MESSENGER, New York City, May 1863

"Let the nativist bigot think and say what he will, the Irish element in America is giving conclusive evidence of devoted attachment to the Union." Northern newspaper, 1862

OPINION IN THE REST OF THE WORLD

Citizens abroad followed news of the war in America and offered a wide range of opinions about the conflict and its outcome.

"The North cannot ever win, and should be stopped before it commits suicide." ESPAÑA, influential Spanish newspaper, 1862

Union soldiers were especially keen to read the papers. One observer described that when a shipment arrived, the men would in unison sink to the ground, and with the rustle of newsprint, devour the latest war news with synchronized motions. Here, a delivery man brings the news.

"Separation [between the North and the South] is not only inevitable, but necessary for the security of European possessions in the New World and for the advance of Spanish prestige in Latin America."

EL DIARIO, prominent Spanish newspaper, 1863

"Sympathy for the North animated all liberal minded Frenchmen from the start. It was in this moment of trial that in France all the friends of liberty recognized each other."

J. S. Mill, writing from Avignon, France

"Americans are cutting each other's throats because one half of them prefer hiring their servants for life, and the other by the hour."

Thomas Carlyle, British writer

"The masses of people all over England—including especially the districts suffering most heavily from the war—are nearly unanimous in sympathizing with the North."

LONDON SPECTATOR, January 1863

"The Southern Confederacy being very difficult of access, the foreigners who have taken service there have all been impelled to do so by their sympathy with the cause, which is in truth a noble one."

Anonymous Austrian Officer

Frank Vizetelly, a British war correspondent.

Covering the War

"To be a spectator was nearly as dangerous as being a participant," artist Edwin Forbes noted about his job as an artist covering the battlefields. At the time of the American Civil War, newspapers did not yet print photographs—although woodcut reproductions were sometimes based on photographs. Forbes was one of the first in the relatively new profession of "war artist," an artist commissioned to bring home images of battle. (Wars would eventually be covered by "combat photographers.") Forbes was joined by other artists, such as Winslow Homer, Theodore Davis, and two British-born brothers, William and Alfred Waud. Their work appeared in prominent Northern publications such as *Leslie's* and *Harper's Weekly*, as well as in international papers such as *The Illustrated London News*.

Most images of battle were sketched on the spot—for example, see Alfred Waud's drawings of

This portrait of Alfred Waud was taken at Gettysburg on July 6, 1863—at the spot that became known as the "Devil's Den." The British-born Waud always carried a revolver and here wore jackboots as he sketched the aftermath of war.

Cold Harbor on page 78. Daring and skilled artists made the war more vivid and real for those far from the battlefront.

SHERMAN'S ATLANTA CAMPAIGN
ATLANTA, GEORGIA, MAY 6–SEPTEMBER 4
UNION VICTORY

Atlanta was one of the most important railroad junctions in the Confederacy, a crossroads filled with stores, foundries, warehouses, and arsenals. Its capture would strike terror in the hearts of civilians and politicians alike. Union General William T. Sherman made Atlanta his chief objective when he left Chattanooga on May 6. The fierce red-bearded warrior was known affectionately as "Uncle Billy" to his men, but he became one of the most hated figures in the Civil War South. Marching toward Atlanta, Sherman carried out the Union policy of total war.

In battles with the Confederate army of General Joseph Johnston, Sherman almost always lost more men than the Confederates, but he kept up his relentless pace. At Kennesaw Mountain, Georgia, on June 27, a Southerner described the Yankee charge: "They seemed to walk up and take death as coolly as if they were automatic or wooden men."

Southern General John Bell Hood—who replaced General Johnston—dug in with his men in Atlanta, but the city was encircled by Union soldiers to the north and east after a daylong battle on July 22. Still, Rebels refused to surrender. Hood's army finally retreated south in September.

A terrified Atlanta woman wrote that Sherman marched in and took "everything and every boddy." She went on to tell that "on the Fourth of September he issued an order exiling the citizens. We were all sent out . . . we were turned out in the woods like cattle." After this evacuation, Sherman set fire to military supplies. When the fires spread, much of Atlanta burned to the ground.

As he rode out of the city early on the morning of November 16 and saw what he had done, Sherman declared, "Behind us lay Atlanta smoldering and in ruins, the black smoke rising high in the air and hanging like a pall over the ruined—and now empty—city."

THE SHENANDOAH VALLEY CAMPAIGN
SHENANDOAH VALLEY, VIRGINIA, MAY–OCTOBER
UNION VICTORY

More than two hundred cadets from the Virginia Military Institute joined the Confederate troops to help hold off Union soldiers moving toward New Market, Virginia, on May 15. Stalled outside Petersburg, Grant had turned his attention to the Shenandoah Valley, threatening to turn it into a "desert" and ordering that "all provisions and stock should be removed and the people notified to get out."

Union General David Hunter, so successful in his conquest of South Carolina the summer before, was given command of a large Union force in Virginia. He marched on Lexington, where he burned down the Virginia Military Institute before pressing on toward Lynchburg.

GENERAL JOSEPH JOHNSTON

EYEWITNESS

AUG. 2. TUESDAY.

We have not been shelled much today, but the muskets have been going all day. I have done but little today but nurse Sister. She has not been well today.

AUG. 3. WEDNESDAY.
This was my birthday. I was ten years old, but I did not have a cake. Times were too hard so I celebrated with ironing. I hope by my next birthday we will have peace in our land so that I can have a nice dinner.

AUG. 5. FRIDAY.
I knit all the morning. In the evening we had to run to Auntie's and get in the cellar. We did not feel safe in our cellar, they fell so thick and fast."

CARRIE BERRY,
a ten-year-old girl
in Atlanta, Georgia,
writing in her diary

Lee ordered General Jubal Early to pursue Hunter with Stonewall Jackson's old corps. The Second Corps of the Army of Virginia tracked Hunter down and eventually chased him and his men into West Virginia. Infuriated, Grant offered General Phil Sheridan command of what became known as the Army of the Shenandoah. In August, Sheridan was ordered to wreck and destroy everything in the valley in his pursuit of Early. This "scorched-earth policy" signaled a harsher aspect of total war and was a crushing blow to civilians. Over the next three months, Sheridan defeated Early's army in three battles and took control of the valley for the Union.

The cat-and-mouse game between Union General Sheridan and Confederate General Early in the valley continued. But by October the Confederates were reduced in number, unable to gather supplies, and tired of fighting a losing battle as they disbanded for winter. The Confederacy's hold on the Shenandoah Valley, which had lasted for most of the war, was finally broken.

The burning and abandoning of Atlanta, one of the South's largest rail centers, was a terrible blow to the Confederates.

Mosby's Rangers

Partisans were soldiers who lived a dangerous life by fighting behind enemy lines, but always in uniform. When Confederate Colonel John Singleton Mosby began his career as a partisan ranger, he had only nine men in his troop, but the numbers soon grew. Tough and resourceful, rangers were trained to gallop past a tree at full speed and drill three bullets into their target. One ranger confessed that they were skilled at "skedaddle," the instinct to know when to retreat following a lightning attack. Mosby gathered eight hundred to two thousand men under his command, operating in northern Virginia and the Shenandoah Valley. Union General Grant made the capture of Mosby a top priority. So successful was Mosby at slipping away from Union soldiers that he became known as the "Gray Ghost."

Detractors called Mosby's Rangers "featherbed soldiers," scoffing that they slept in comfort while "real soldiers" roughed it. In fact, partisans were more likely to rough it—hiding in the woods and sleeping on leaves under poles covered with cornstalks known as "shebangs."

Mosby's success made him one of the few Confederates below the rank of general to capture headlines in the Northern press. Nevertheless, he was secretive about his strategies, boasting that "only three men in the Confederate Army knew what I was doing or intended to do."

Union commander Thomas Ewing, the brother-in-law of William T. Sherman, was in charge of western Missouri, where he had to battle outlaw forces headed by notorious Confederate bandits William Quantrill and "Bloody Bill" Anderson. These guerrillas, or outlaw soldiers, encouraged Rebel commanders to believe that the people in Missouri would overthrow Union rule.

Confederate General Sterling Price invaded Missouri from the South with 12,000 men and met little resistance until he encountered Ewing's Union troops. Ewing's force of only 1,000 managed to inflict huge losses on Price's army of nearly 7,000. When the Confederate general lost more than a quarter of his men, he was forced to turn westward away from his objective, the city of St. Louis.

In October Price's men fought several Union divisions near Kansas City. Again, strong Yankee resistance drove Price back, so the Confederate general was forced to retreat over the Arkansas border within two short months. He brought back fewer than 6,000 troops. In the aftermath, "Bloody Bill" Anderson was dead and William Quantrill fled eastward, vowing to assassinate Lincoln. Quantrill was killed by a Union patrol in Kentucky, Missouri remained within the Union, and 70 percent of the voters supported Lincoln in his reelection.

DID YOU KNOW?

Union soldiers were issued coffee beans that they had to grind themselves. But "instant coffee" was an experiment for Union soldiers. Coffee was blended with cream and sugar, then reduced to paste form and distributed to Yankee troops—to be dissolved in boiling water and drunk as a hot beverage.

Quantrill's Raiders

Confederate raiders along the Kansas-Missouri border gained fame under the leadership of proslavery guerrilla William Clarke Quantrill, ringleader of the gangs who lawlessly prowled the war's western edges. Despite Union threats, wives and sisters of Quantrill's men offered shelter and assistance to the outlaw rebels. After Union commander Thomas Ewing rounded up these women, the building where they were held collapsed, and five women were killed. Quantrill's men demanded revenge, and a force of nearly five hundred stormed across the

The burning of Lawrence, Kansas, by Quantrill's raiders.

border into Kansas to kidnap and execute ten farmers. Quantrill raided Lawrence on August 21, 1863, issuing the order: "Kill every man and burn every house." Within three hours almost two hundred men and boys were dead and nearly two hundred buildings were destroyed by fire.

Then Union General Ewing issued his infamous Order 11, which forced all citizens out of four Missouri counties, banishing ten thousand people from their homes. Order 11 enraged those living on the border, and the region became one of the war's most dangerous areas.

Food and Rations

Feeding the great armies of the North and South was one of the most difficult tasks of wartime. Many soldiers had a hard time getting used to the mealtime fare. Charles Nott, a sixteen-year-old from New York, complained of his supper on a freezing evening: "It consisted of hard bread, raw pork and coffee. The coffee you probably would not recognize in New York. Boiled in an open kettle, and about the color of a brownstone front, it was nevertheless . . . the only warm thing we had. The pork was frozen, and the water in the canteens solid ice, so we had to hold them over the fire when we wanted a drink."

Most endured meager diets, as one boy reported: "Rations at last; one course meal—cracker and a small bit of bacon: one ration. We are informed that these rations were issued in advance for the following twenty-four hours. Useless to protest. . . ."

In army camps, independent peddlers known as sutlers traveled with their portable stores and charged high prices for food. Eggs, butter, and sugar, once easy to obtain, were now luxuries. One young boy excitedly described arriving in a town where he could enjoy a treat: "I ran into a store, got hold of a tin wash pan, drew it full of molasses, got a box of good Yankee crackers, sat down on the ground in a vacant lot, dipped the crackers into the molasses, and ate the best meal I ever had."

Both armies usually forbade soldiers to forage, to take food from civilians, but many bent the rules to supplement their diets. Most soldiers would dig up produce in gardens and perhaps even steal a chicken or a cow. Soldier John Delhaney described raids on beehives, which yielded great delicacies. But these opportunities were rare for soldiers on the march.

CAMP LINGO

bummers: soldiers who scavenged the countryside looking for food

butternuts: Rebel soldiers (from the dye sometimes used in the South for Confederate uniforms)

A BUMMER

bully soup: cornmeal, hardtack, wine, ginger, and water cooked together

Company Q: anyone requesting sick leave

cush: bacon, corn bread, and water cooked together

gaiters: leather covering for legs

haversack: canvas or cloth bag with a strap to carry rations

housewife: a soldier's sewing kit

kepi: a cap

pard: a soldier's best friend

skedaddle: to run away from battle

sutler: civilian merchant following the army

tanglefoot, old red-eye, or pop skull: liquor

wagon dogs: soldiers faking illness to ride on wagons

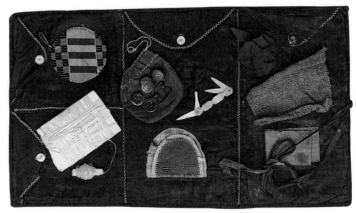

A HOUSEWIFE

O ver the course of the summer, Lincoln's friends and advisors feared that even if he won the nomination of his own Republican party, he could be defeated in the autumn election. Many worried that the Republicans might even choose another candidate.

Northerners had lost faith in their president for many reasons—resentment of the draft, high taxes, and general war weariness. Lincoln's political enemies accused him of despotism, claiming that he acted like a dictator. Members of his own party doubted that he could continue the job. However, Lincoln won the Republican nomination and strengthened his chances for reelection by inviting Andrew Johnson of Tennessee to join him on the ticket as vice president

Lincoln faced strong competition from his main opponent, Democratic party candidate General George B. McClellan. Known affectionately to his soldiers as "Little Mac," McClellan was a popular campaigner, and vowed to end the war with honor to both sides. Having commanded one of the largest Union field

ABOVE: **Sketch by William Waud of Union soldiers voting near Petersburg.**
RIGHT: **"Long Lincoln," a caricature of the president from** *Harper's Weekly.*

armies in 1861, McClellan was clearly not a pacifist. But he had often been slow to advance into battle, though he blamed Union defeats on Lincoln's lack of strategy and leadership. Thirty-eight-year-old McClellan was young and dynamic, an impressive candidate to oppose the gaunt and aging Lincoln.

The president's advisors urged him to give soldiers leaves to go home so they could vote. Indeed, the votes from the military, as well as the stunning capture of Atlanta before the election, turned the results in Lincoln's favor. The president carried all states remaining in the Union except Kentucky, Delaware, and New Jersey. He won 212 electoral votes to McClellan's 21. At the same time, the popular vote was extremely close: Lincoln carried New York by less than 7,000 votes out of the 730,000 cast. However, voter turnout in 1864 was larger than in 1860, making his reelection a strong show of approval.

There were those who still wanted Lincoln to call a truce and negotiate. But the president was convinced that his administration would be given the opportunity to end the war, defeat the Confederacy, and "maintain the integrity of the Union."

A pro-Lincoln cartoon depicting the Democratic candidate McClellan with a spade. As a military leader, McClellan "dug in" when Lincoln urged him to combat.

Finding a Southern Running Mate

When Lincoln was seeking reelection, not only did he want to strengthen his chances of winning, but he also looked ahead to a time when the war would be over. He considered a future when all people, North and South, would set aside their differences and be reunited. For that reason, he asked his vice president, Hannibal Hamlin of Maine, who was a strong Yankee presence and a reminder of the antislavery origins of the Republican party, to step down. To demonstrate his firm commitment to unity, Lincoln chose a Southerner for his running mate. Indeed, Lincoln picked Andrew

ANDREW JOHNSON

Johnson of Tennessee, the only Southern senator who had not resigned his seat when secession divided the nation and war broke out. Though Confederates despised Johnson for his Union sympathies, he was nevertheless both a loyal Unionist and a Southerner. Lincoln hoped that this Southerner would be able to reach out to his countrymen when the time came. Johnson was not a popular or well-known figure in Washington, but he was a symbol that North and South must begin the healing process, and that Lincoln was ready to start it with his second run for the presidency.

SAND CREEK MASSACRE
SAND CREEK, COLORADO, NOVEMBER 29

The disruptions of war aroused conflicts among Indian nations and pitched battles between the federal government and different tribes. In November 1864, war between the Cheyenne and Arapaho nations left Denver, Colorado, isolated and unprotected. Indian raids against gold miners in the West were on the rise, and Union soldiers, blaming the Cheyenne, decided to attack one of their settlements. The troops wanted to retaliate against Native American attacks, which the soldiers felt undermined the Union cause.

On November 29, 1864, perhaps the most horrible massacre of the war took place along a small creek in Colorado. Union troops—mostly Colorado volunteers—descended on the Cheyenne encampment near Sand Creek and slaughtered one-third of the villagers. The death toll included dozens of women and children, even babies slain in their mother's arms. Nearly four hundred fifty Indians died in the attack, which had been ordered by Colonel J. M. Chivington of the Colorado militia. The federal government condemned this shameful episode, but the Sand Creek Massacre, as it has become known, is a painful reminder of the suffering inflicted on Native Americans throughout the century, even while the country was at war.

> ### BATTLE AT-A-GLANCE
>
> **BATTLE OF NASHVILLE**
> **Nashville, Tennessee,**
> **December 15–16**
>
> Union troops: 55,000
> Confederate troops: 30,000
>
> Union casualties: 3,000
> Confederate casualties: 6,000
> **UNION VICTORY**

BATTLE OF NASHVILLE

Union General George Thomas and his 55,000 men had turned Nashville, Tennessee, into an armed camp. Bloodied in a brave but foolish charge at nearby Franklin, Confederate General Hood's 23,000 men stood on the high ground above Nashville, hoping to lure Thomas into battle. Grant ordered Thomas to attack, but sleet interrupted his planned assault.

Grant was impatient and was almost ready to replace Thomas. But on the morning of December 15, as a dense fog rolled in, Thomas sent a unit of black troops to attack the Confederates on the side and ordered another infantry unit to attack Hood's center. All day and all night the men fought, unwilling to give up ground. Confederate cavalry under the command of General Nathan Bedford Forrest held off Union troops so that 15,000 Confederates escaped capture, but the Yankees were still able to take 4,500 prisoners. It was a stunning defeat for the proud Rebel army.

Confederate General Hood had suffered terrible losses, and his Army of Tennessee lay in ruins. Humiliated, Hood was replaced with General Johnston. The last great encounter between blue and gray in the West was over.

A Confederate soldier.

Spies

During wartime the Union War Department hired detective Allan Pinkerton to find "all suspect persons" in the District of Columbia. Pinkerton expanded the scope of his investigations considerably and hired "operatives" to gather intelligence throughout the South. One such daring agent, Timothy Webster, was spying on the Confederate army in Tennessee when he was nearly

unmasked. Those caught and convicted faced execution, and Webster had to leap onto a moving train to escape discovery. Webster's spying in Richmond led to the arrest of a Confederate agent in the U.S. Provost Marshal's office.

ALLAN PINKERTON (SEATED AT RIGHT)

Some of the most daring spies on both sides were women. After she was captured by the Union government, Confederate agent Belle Boyd was able to flee to Canada and avoid prosecution when her jailer fell in love with her and allowed her to escape. A celebrated Washington society hostess named Rose Greenhow was arrested after the Confederate victory at Bull Run, because the Union learned that she had smuggled information to Southern generals that contributed to their victory. Greenhow was eventually released and ran the blockade to Europe. She was smuggling

funds and documents back to President Davis when her ship ran into a Union patrol. Though she tried to row ashore to avoid capture, her boat capsized and she drowned, weighed down by the gold coins sewn into her gown.

BELLE BOYD

Elizabeth Van Lew, a Richmond woman loyal to the Union, was able to place her former slave, a free black woman named Mary Elizabeth Bowser, as a spy within the Jefferson Davis home. Bowser passed along information she gathered from Davis's desk at the Confederate White House, and Van Lew scribbled messages in code on dress patterns and smuggled them north. Another spy, Pauline Cushman, was a New Orleans-born actress who acted as a double agent. She played the role of a Confederate sympathizer, but passed secrets to Union officers.

These women are just a handful of the scores of agents for both sides who obtained vital information during the war. The battles were fought not only on fields of combat. Working behind enemy lines, dozens of men and women spies risked their lives for their beliefs.

ROSE GREENHOW

After his bold conquest of Atlanta earlier in the year, General Sherman hoped to cut a wide path across Georgia, crushing civilians into submission and driving the Rebel army out. Lincoln wanted Sherman to wait until after the presidential election to make his "March to the Sea," so Sherman spent more than two months in and around Atlanta before heading east on November 16.

Cut off from all communications with Washington and Grant, Sherman vowed, "I can make Georgia howl." Howl its people did, as the Union commander maintained a steady pace of 15 miles a day, allowing his men plenty of time to destroy rail lines, plunder stock and poultry, raid pantries, and commit mayhem along the way. Sherman's artillery units melted down and twisted the iron rods broken away from railroad tracks, littering the country with destroyed rail lines that became known as "Sherman's hairpins." A belt of Georgia 50 miles wide was swept clean of all food and supplies.

The Union troops destroyed an arsenal at Milledgeville, leaving a trail of debris and bad feelings behind. And when federal soldiers encountered Union prisoners who had escaped from the Confederate prison at Andersonville, Sherman's men became even more vengeful and violent. Civilians, especially women and children alone on isolated farmsteads, were terrified that their homes would be sacked and plundered by "bummers," or undisciplined soldiers. Families buried their silver and jewelry to protect them from advancing Yankee hordes. Many Confederates lost their heirlooms, photos, and keepsakes, and watched all their belongings go up in smoke.

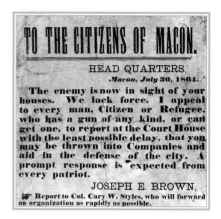

TO THE CITIZENS OF MACON.

HEAD QUARTERS,
Macon, July 30, 1864.

The enemy is now in sight of your houses. We lack force. I appeal to every man, Citizen or Refugee, who has a gun of any kind, or can get one, to report at the Court House with the least possible delay, that you may be thrown into Companies and aid in the defense of the city. A prompt response is expected from every patriot.

JOSEPH E. BROWN.

Report to Col. Cary W. Styles, who will forward an organization as rapidly as possible.

The Yankee invasion of Georgia caused alarmed Confederates to call citizens to arms.

Union soldiers tore up the railroad and melted iron ties into twisted metal to keep Confederates from repairing the rail lines. These twisted shapes littered the Southern landscape, grim reminders of Union destruction.

Southern refugees fled before Union General William T. Sherman's invading army.

Rebel troops retreated east to Savannah, but the Union general easily defeated a Southern force at Fort McAllister, the town's main defense. The remaining Confederate troops evacuated before the Union army pushed across the Savannah River to occupy the town. On December 22 Sherman wired President Lincoln his good news: "I beg to present you, as a Christmas gift, the city of Savannah."

NEW YEAR'S RESOLUTIONS

As the iron grip of the Union tightened on the Confederacy, survival seemed less and less likely. Although the officers were willing to continue their command of the Rebel army, and the soldiers in gray fought on valiantly, Southern civilians and soldiers prayed for their deliverance from war as intensely as their leaders longed for independence.

Lincoln's generals had delivered staggering military blows to the South over the course of the year. After the onset of "total war," which cut supply lines and starved civilians, the Union command believed the South would accept defeat before much more time passed.

For Jefferson Davis, time seemed to be running out. The West was securely in Union hands. Grant had encircled Petersburg. Sherman had conquered central and coastal Georgia, striking hard and deep in the heart of Dixie. Though the South still hoped to hang on to Richmond, the North rallied behind Lincoln's plan to end the war on Union terms. The President wanted to force the Confederacy to give up, once and for all, and to restore the South to the Union.

EYEWITNESS

"About three miles from Sparta we struck the 'burnt country,' as it is well named by the natives, and then I could better understand the wrath and desperation of these poor people. I almost felt as if I should like to hang a Yankee myself. . . . The dwellings that were standing all showed signs of pillage, and on every plantation we saw the charred remains of the ginhouse and packing screw, while here and there lone chimney stacks, 'Sherman's sentinels,' told of homes laid in ashes. . . ."

ELIZA ANDREWS, a young girl in Georgia, reporting what she saw after Sherman's army had marched through

"War, like a thunderbolt, follows its laws and turns not aside, even if the beautiful, the virtuous, and the charitable stand in its path."

GENERAL WILLIAM T. SHERMAN

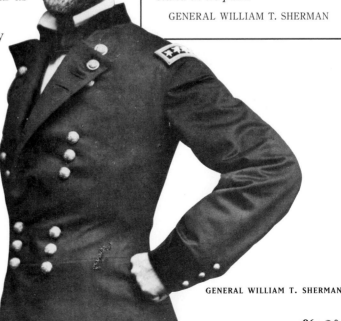

GENERAL WILLIAM T. SHERMAN

CHAPTER 6

1865

AND AFTER

hen General Robert E. Lee surrendered at Appomattox Courthouse, Virginia, in April 1865, Americans hoped that the killing had ended. However, hopes for a smooth transition to peace were cut short when an assassin shot the President on April 14 at Ford's Theater in Washington—only five days after Lee's surrender. Lincoln's death shocked the nation, as North and South came together to try to bind the wounds of war.

The transition to peace was even more difficult under the leadership of Andrew Johnson, despised by Southerners for siding with the Union and distrusted by the Union for being a Southerner.

During the era immediately following the war, the period known as Reconstruction, the federal government readmitted Southern states to the Union. Republican leaders pushed through legislation giving African Americans citizenship rights and stationed soldiers in the South to enforce the new laws. During this tumultuous period, Southern state governments resisted Yankee rule. Former Confederates faced the monumental challenge of overcoming the hardships and losses they had suffered, while at the same time, blacks in the South struggled for equality. The question of gains and losses, the debates over rights and equality, stirred passions long after the Civil War ended and still provoke debates today.

Richmond, the Confederate capital, lay in ruins at the end of the war. Mills and docks were destroyed by the heavy fighting and Yankee invasion.

1865 AND AFTER AT-A-GLANCE

January
Thirteenth Amendment

March 4
Lincoln's Second Inaugural

April 9
Surrender at Appomattox Courthouse, Virginia

April 14
Lincoln's Assassination

1866
Fourteenth Amendment

1868
President Johnson's Impeachment

1870
Fifteenth Amendment

1877
Withdrawal of federal troops from the South—end of Reconstruction

THIRTEENTH AMENDMENT
JANUARY 31, 1865

The amendment to the Constitution abolishing slavery was Lincoln's most lasting triumph. Many Democrats in Congress opposed the measure, fearing that the South would never agree to return to the Union without slavery. But Congress voted an end to slavery by the two-thirds majority required for constitutional amendments. On January 31, when the Thirteenth Amendment won by a narrow margin, victorious legislators wept and cheered. Blacks, who had only recently been allowed to sit in the galleries of the Capitol, joined in the jubilation.

FREEDMEN'S BUREAU
MARCH 3, 1865

Congress established the Bureau of Refugees, Freedmen and Abandoned Lands (commonly known as the Freedmen's Bureau) shortly after the passage of the Thirteenth Amendment. The purpose of this group was to provide food, medical care, education, and other assistance to homeless and destitute freed people throughout the South.

The bureau was headed by the one-armed Union General Oliver O. Howard (after whom Howard University of Washington, D.C., was named). He sent agents all over the occupied South to create schools, provide legal services, and enforce federal law. Many of these enterprises were supported by private Northern charities, as Yankee teachers by the hundreds went south to help with the more than three thousand schools established. Freedmen's Bureau agents were dedicated to the task of helping blacks support themselves in the war-torn states, although they were helpless when former slaves wanted to remain to farm the lands on which they had always lived. Congress refused to allow black families to seize the property of former Confederates.

Laura Towne, one of the many hundreds of Yankee women who went south to educate the freed people after the war. Towne founded the Penn School on the South Carolina Sea Island of St. Helena.

A freedmen's school, where children and adults attended classes to learn to read and write after slavery was abolished.

Lincoln's Second Inaugural

The crowd that gathered to see Lincoln take his oath of office on a cold, windy inaugural day was treated to a spectacular sight: the newly completed dome of the U.S. Capitol, crowned by a bronze statute representing Liberty. Standing in the shadow of this crowning Liberty, Lincoln pledged to be merciful in his dealings with the South: "With malice toward none, with charity for all; with firmness in the right, as God gives us to see the right, let us strive on to finish the work we are in; to bind up the nation's wounds. . . ."

After his address Lincoln remarked that he was exhausted, thinking that he might be "the tiredest man on earth." Having carried so many burdens while in the White House, having seen the nation through its darkest days, Lincoln hoped he would soon be refreshed, if not by victory, then by an end to the terrible plague of war.

Lincoln aged considerably during his first term in office, as seen by comparing this portrait from 1865 with the one on page 24, taken in 1860.

Crowds gathered to witness the President taking the inaugural oath for a second time.

SHERMAN IN THE CAROLINAS, FEBRUARY

"Here is where the treason began and, by God, here is where it shall end!" a Union soldier declared, as Sherman decided to head from Georgia into South Carolina. Lee's army was the only Confederate force of any size and strength left in the field, and his supplies came from the Carolinas. Forced to cross more than nine rivers and hundreds of miles of hostile swamps, Sherman cut right through the middle of South Carolina, capturing the capital, Columbia, on February 17.

By the next day, half the town had been destroyed. Confederates complained that Union troops recklessly torched the city, and Yankees declared that the Southern soldiers had caused the fire by burning cotton bales before they fled. Regardless of who started the fire, the town was in ashes and Sherman headed for North Carolina.

Sherman's army left South Carolina in ruins.

FALL OF RICHMOND, APRIL 3, 1865

Throughout the chill, damp spring Lee watched his army of fifty thousand slowly dwindle. Many Confederates headed home to plant, not wanting to spend another springtime at war. Still Grant and Lee battered away at each other until Lee was forced to retreat from Petersburg, leaving Richmond vulnerable.

Lee sent a wire to President Jefferson Davis, who received the warning about the approaching Union troops while he was worshiping in church. As soon as civilians heard the news, they began to flee the city.

Lincoln was in Petersburg on April 3, when he received word that Richmond was in Union hands. The president confessed, "Thank God I have lived to see this. It seems to me that I have been dreaming a horrid dream for four years, and now the nightmare is gone. I want to see Richmond." Admiral David Porter took the president upriver by boat to see the Rebel capital.

The lanky president insisted upon walking the streets. His guards feared for his safety, but Lincoln was soon surrounded by a crowd of grateful blacks who reached out to him, dropped to their knees in prayer, and warmly embraced the Union leader. The entire scene was one of celebration, for both the freed slaves and the man they called "Father Abraham." Back in Washington, news of the fall of Richmond prompted an 800-gun salute!

DID YOU KNOW?

When a shell exploded in his kitchen as the two great armies clashed near his farm at the First Battle of Bull Run in July 1861, Wilmer McLean, a Southern planter, moved his family far away to safety. But history seemed to follow him, and in April 1865 Grant and Lee met in his new home in Appomattox Courthouse to settle the terms of surrender. McLean boasted in truth: "The war began in my front yard and ended in my front parlor."

Surrender at Appomattox

While Lincoln was realizing his dreams by visiting Richmond, Robert E. Lee felt as though his entire world was slipping away. Union forces were closing in on him as he tried to fight his way past the approaching enemy.

In Danville, Virginia, fleeing from the Union army, Jefferson Davis tried to rally his people: "Relieved from the necessity of guarding the cities . . . with our army free to move from point to point . . . nothing is now needed to render our triumph certain, but . . . our own unquenchable resolve." But when the Union forces captured six thousand of Lee's men and destroyed his supply train on April 6, the Confederate general knew the end was at hand.

An artist's fanciful interpretation of Lee and Grant's meeting at Appomattox Courthouse. In fact, the two did not sit down together, but were at separate tables during negotiations.

The next day Grant sent a white flag to Lee and a note requesting a truce. For the first time ever, Robert E. Lee asked about terms. Tension mounted on April 8 when it seemed that the Confederate general might try to rally his men for one last stand. Instead, the Confederate commander agreed to surrender.

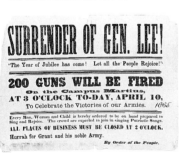

The two generals met in the home of Wilmer McLean in Appomattox Courthouse, Virginia, to negotiate terms. Lee arrived in full-dress uniform with a decorated sword, while Grant wore his regular uniform, muddy boots, and no sword. Grant was generous with terms. According to the offer, Rebel officers and men were free to go home. Lee asked Grant to allow his soldiers to take their own horses home, and Grant agreed. After the surrender, Grant generously sent three days rations to the twenty-five thousand defeated and starving Confederate soldiers. Although happy about the surrender, Grant remarked that he was saddened "at the downfall of a foe who had fought so long and valiantly."

Reports of surrender at Appomattox were discredited by many Southerners who could not believe that Lee would ever give up the fight. But soon, Confederates had to accept defeat.

Despite Lee's actions, General Joseph Johnston did not surrender in North Carolina until April 26, and General Kirby Smith kept fighting until May 26, when he surrendered the Confederate armies west of the Mississippi River. Less than two months after the treaty at Appomattox, the Confederates became a conquered people.

Even Confederate President Davis had been captured in Georgia on May 10. Union soldiers seized Davis, put him in shackles, and dragged him back to prison. He was imprisoned for two years, unable to see his family.

A newspaper image of the capture of Jefferson Davis, allegedly wearing women's clothing as a disguise.

News of Lee's surrender caused celebration in most of Washington, but not for Rebel spies who felt betrayed. Though most accepted the end of the war, some wanted to plunge the nation back into bloodshed and chaos. A band of Confederate agents, headed by actor John Wilkes Booth, conspired to assassinate Lincoln and members of his cabinet. By doing so, they hoped to topple the Union government and return Jefferson Davis to power.

On Good Friday evening, April 14, while President and Mrs. Lincoln attended a play at Ford's Theater in Washington, D.C., John Wilkes Booth slipped into the president's box, fired a shot into Lincoln's head, leapt onto the stage shouting, *"Sic semper tyrannis"* (so be it always to tyrants), and fled into the night. The theater echoed with screams of terror. Lincoln was carried into a private home nearby, where surrounded by his family and friends, he died early the next morning. The news of his murder spread through the country on Easter weekend.

Lincoln's funeral procession.

John Wilkes Booth

Born into a famous theatrical family, John Wilkes Booth was the younger brother of the Shakespearean actor Edwin Booth and the son of a British Shakespearean actor. When John Wilkes Booth became an actor in the 1850s, he was following in impressive footsteps. Booth flirted with a military career, although when the Civil War broke out he did not enlist. However, he was a staunch Confederate sympathizer who continued to live in the Union capital, Washington. Besides performing, he involved himself in secret espionage activities on behalf of the Confederates. He was allegedly part of a network of agents working out of the District of Columbia who undertook extensive operations in the North and Canada. Near the end of the war, Booth was in charge of a plot to kidnap Lincoln. His secret cell, or group, of Confederate operatives planned to snatch Lincoln and hold him for ransom, which they hoped would end the fighting and secure Confederate independence. Booth and his men shadowed the president's every move, scheming to take him during one of his frequent afternoon outings on horseback. When Lee surrendered before they were able to attempt the kidnapping, Booth's co-conspirators decided to assassinate Lincoln and key officials in his cabinet. Booth especially wanted to seize the moment and save the day for the Confederacy. He was only twenty-six when he died.

BOOTH CONSPIRACY AND TRIAL

The train carrying Lincoln's body home to Springfield, Illinois, for burial.

While Booth was attacking Lincoln, his co-conspirator Lewis Powell, known as Lewis Payne, forced his way into the home of Secretary of State Seward and stabbed him several times—but Seward survived. Other conspirators were scheduled to attack other major figures, but failed to reach General Ulysses S. Grant and Vice President Andrew Johnson.

Secretary of War Edwin Stanton declared martial law and organized one of the largest manhunts in American history to catch Booth and his co-conspirators. On April 26 the assassin was trapped in a burning barn in rural Maryland, along with one of his accomplices. Booth was shot and killed. His body was returned to Washington in secret and buried in a storeroom in a warehouse. The federal government did not want Booth to have a funeral and become a martyr or hero to the South, so officials refused to release his body to the Booth family.

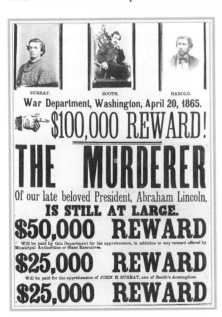

The search for John Wilkes Booth in 1865 was the nation's largest manhunt ever, as thousands sought the assassin.

Eight conspirators were put on trial for the murder of the president. The government demanded a speedy trial, promising to punish the guilty, restore order, and put the matter to rest as soon as possible. Mary Surratt, who owned the boardinghouse where the plotters met was among the four who were hanged. Seeing a woman put to death shocked the American people. Four others, including Dr. Samuel Mudd, who had treated Booth's leg (which he injured while jumping onto the stage during his getaway at Ford's Theater), were sent to prison. The government hoped that the execution and imprisonment of the assassination conspirators would close a terrible and violent episode of American history.

EYEWITNESS

"The 15th day of April [Lincoln's death] will be a day forever memorable in history by an act of atrocity that has no parallel in the annals of men. . . . Hereafter, through all time, wherever the Black Race may be known in the world; whenever and wherever it shall lay the foundations of power; build its cities and rear its temples, it will sacredly preserve if not deify the name of 'Abraham, the Martyr.'"

DR. S. W. ROGERS, an African American, responding to Lincoln's assassination in an editorial in the New Orleans *Black Republican*

When he was sworn in as president, Johnson knew what a difficult task he faced. He pursued a mild course of action in his dealings with the Confederates, which angered many Republicans in Congress. Johnson claimed he was only fulfilling Lincoln's wish to be merciful and to restore the Union rapidly and without hostility. But because Johnson was a Southerner, Northern congressmen suspected his motives.

Even though the Southern economy was shattered, most former slave owners returned to their plantations, where they found conditions harsh but where they hoped to rebuild their lives.

The planters who remained in the South hoped to assert authority over black labor and limit economic opportunities for African Americans. States like Louisiana passed "Black Codes," which restricted the freedom of African Americans. These state laws were struck down by the federal government.

Confederates were upset by both "carpetbaggers" and "scalawags." "Carpetbaggers" (named for the traveling bags they carried) were black or white Northerners who moved south to take advantage of the opportunities of Republican rule in the former Confederate states. "Scalawags" were perhaps even more despised because they were former Confederates who cooperated in business and politics with federal authorities. Southerners also resented the presence of federal soldiers who treated them like a conquered nation.

Angered by former Confederates' stubborn resistance to federal laws, Congress was fed up with these "proud, bloated and defiant" ex-Confederates, as Republican House leader Thaddeus Stevens called them.

In 1866 a civil rights act, which President Johnson tried to veto, granted former slaves citizenship. Also in 1866 Congress passed the Fourteenth Amendment, which defined national citizenship to include former slaves. In the November Congressional elections, Radical Republicans won a large majority. Congress demanded that the president accept its Reconstruction program.

A carpetbag, a nineteenth-century suitcase, was the traditional symbol of the Yankee who came south for financial gain after the Civil War.

Andrew Johnson

Born in 1808 in Raleigh, North Carolina, into a humble family who later moved to Tennessee, Johnson was an illiterate tailor until his wife taught him to read and write. He served in the House of Representatives for ten years and the governor's mansion of Tennessee for eight years before being elected to the U.S. Senate in 1857. Following secession, Johnson was the only Southern senator to remain loyal to the Union. Lincoln valued his support and rewarded him with the number-two spot on the presidential ticket in 1864. But Vice President Johnson was ill-prepared to assume the office of president when Lincoln was assassinated. Johnson's temperament caused numerous misunderstandings: Congressional leaders thought he was "soft" on former Confederates and too liberal with presidential pardons. His clashes with Congress led to his impeachment hearings in 1868. Although he was not removed from office, Johnson left the office of the presidency in disgrace.

Captain Henry Wirz and Andersonville Prison

During the last year of the war, increasing numbers of Yankee prisoners were shipped to an open stockade on 27 acres near Macon, Georgia, that became known as Andersonville Prison. The stockade was enclosed by 20-foot-high pine walls in an area of swampland with a stream 5 feet wide and a foot deep running through it. The men were poorly housed in tents. At times more than thirty thousand prisoners were held at Andersonville, making it the fifth-largest city in the Confederacy.

The prisoners suffered from hunger, thirst, lice, fevers, and scurvy. Typhus, typhoid, and other plagues swept through the prison yard, and no medicines were available. Starvation contributed to the death toll, which reached three thousand per month in late spring and summer, when overcrowding was at its worst. In September 1864, Confederate doctor Joseph Jones reported that the place was one "gigantic mass of human misery." More than forty-nine thousand Union soldiers were sent to Andersonville in the last year of the war, and more than one in four was buried there.

The hanging of Captain Henry Wirz.

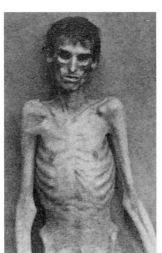

The Union prisoners were reduced to skin and bones. Images such as this stimulated Northern cries for revenge against Confederates like Wirz.

After the war, the public outcry over Andersonville was enormous. The Swiss-American Confederate commandant of the prison, Henry Wirz, was indicted for "war crimes." By the time of the trial, Wirz was an invalid and had to lie on a couch in the courtroom, as he protested that he was innocent. Wirz claimed to have done his best under the awful conditions of war and noted that thousands of Confederate soldiers had died in Union prison camps. The Union military court tried him and condemned him to death. Many people argued that Wirz was a scapegoat, but others claimed that his harsh policies caused countless deaths that might have been avoided. When he was hanged on November 10, 1865, Wirz became the first and only Confederate officer executed for war crimes.

By 1867 Radical Republicans had decided to show the former Rebel states who was boss. On March 2, Congress divided the South into five military districts. The only way a state could be readmitted to the Union was to pledge to obey federal laws and to guarantee former slave men the vote. Southerners did not want to obey these rules, but U.S. soldiers were stationed in the South to enforce the laws. President Johnson objected to the way Congress wanted to run Reconstruction.

At the same time, Congress passed laws prohibiting presidential action without legislative approval. President Johnson believed that Congress was overstepping its boundaries and tried to overrule Congress. Johnson's defiance of Congress resulted in his "impeachment." The President was charged with disobeying the Constitution and put on trial. If he lost, he could be removed from office.

Johnson was the first president to be tried in the United States Senate. After three ballots, he was found innocent of the charges on May 26, 1868. However, in the November elections, the Republicans turned Johnson out and replaced him with the former military hero Ulysses S. Grant, who easily won the presidency and took office in 1869.

STRUGGLES FOR BLACK FREEDOM

In 1875 Congress passed another civil rights act, which prohibited states from keeping blacks off juries and from excluding them from public places such as hotels, public transportation, and theaters. But former Confederates tried to promote white supremacy, claiming that blacks were inferior and should be kept "in their place."

In 1866 members of a group known as the Ku Klux Klan made Confederate war hero and former general Nathan Bedford Forrest their first leader. The Klan, whose name is from the Greek word *kuklos,* meaning "circle," was named after the social club in Pulaski, Tennessee, where the organization was founded. Its members used violence and terror to advance their white supremacist views.

In 1870 the federal government passed the Fifteenth Amendment, which stated that the right to vote could not be denied by "any State on account of race, color, or previous condition of servitude." In response, the Klan fought back.

Blacks who sought an education, tried to buy land, or cast a ballot often risked their lives. Scores of Southern blacks were beaten, wounded, and even murdered for claiming their legal rights.

INSET: **A freedman casting his first vote, in an illustration from** *Harper's Weekly.*

Two Alabama members of the Ku Klux Klan. Often these vigilantes were called "Night Riders" because they would make their raids by moonlight, wearing hoods to disguise their identity as they threatened and intimidated political enemies, especially freedmen asserting their civil rights.

Sharecroppers hoped to divide the profits from a harvest at the end of the year with the landowner.

"FORTY ACRES AND A MULE"

Many former slaves believed the federal government should help them on the long, hard road to freedom. But most felt, as one former slave declared, that they were given "nothing but freedom."

During Reconstruction, many African Americans tried to find lost family members—to restore children to parents, husbands to wives, and others to families separated by slave sales and refugee life. Many Southern blacks hoped to achieve real independence, but knew they had little chance unless they could work their own land and become self-sufficient.

When the Union army seized Confederate estates during the war, the soldiers sometimes allowed former slaves to work the land for themselves. But once the Civil War ended, the land was returned to former white owners.

Rumors circulated that the federal government would give former slaves "forty acres and a mule," which would have been an important first step for African Americans. But debates in Congress grew more heated. The right to vote, rather than the right to land, took center stage.

Most blacks in the South were forced to return to plantations as paid workers or as sharecroppers. Owners provided sharecroppers, also known as tenant farmers, with housing, tools, seed, and other supplies. Blacks supplied the labor to plant the crop. At harvest, owners paid the workers with shares of the crops rather than in wages. Although many freedmen were initially hopeful about the potential rewards of sharecropping, most blacks remained impoverished or in debt under the system. Only a very small portion were able to save enough money to buy their own land. African Americans who were able to start schools and build businesses in the South pushed open the door of opportunity, seeking a little bit more, then a little bit more again and struggling for equality. But most African Americans were not given a fair chance to compete in the postwar South.

Confederates in Exile

"All I wish & long for is to get out of reach of it all—just to go anywhere—Brazil, Australia, or anywhere else. I believe we could be comparatively happy when once out of sight and hearing of these Yankees," wrote Confederate Louisa McCord Smythe from Charleston, South Carolina, following surrender. Like thousands of other former slave owners, Smythe wanted to escape Yankee rule. In the summer and fall of 1865, hundreds of Southern families left the country. Confederate exiles established a large colony in Brazil, where the government welcomed American expatriates. Some of these "Confederados," as the exiles were known, still preserve their Southern heritage in communities of descendants who live in South America today.

Not all foreign colonies did well. General Sterling Price took a large group of Confederates with him to Mexico to found the Carlotta Colony. Although Mexico had abolished slavery, these Confederates were allowed to bring along their slaves. This exile community, like similar ones in Venezuela, did not survive. Price and his followers eventually returned to the United States.

Other Confederate aristocrats crossed the border to settle in southern Canada. When he was released from prison in 1867, Jefferson Davis was reunited with his wife and children in Canada. Louisa McCord Smythe's own mother, unable to tolerate Yankee rule in South Carolina, retreated there, but returned to the South after 1877.

During Reconstruction, blacks won seats in Congress for the first time in American history. Sixteen African Americans served in the House of Representatives and two in the Senate. Most African Americans were willing to endure the insults and even physical attacks that followed when they assumed political office during this tumultuous time.

Many of the black men who took office were well educated and prepared for officeholding. Francis Louis Cardozo graduated from the University of Glasgow in Scotland and went on to become the principal of Charleston, South Carolina's, Avery Institute. He served as secretary of state for South Carolina (1868–72) and state treasurer (1872–77). The Reverend Richard H. Cain was elected to two terms in Congress (1873–75, 1877–79), before he retired to become an African Methodist Episcopal bishop. Hiram Revels, a graduate of Knox College in Illinois, became the provost marshal of Vicksburg, Mississippi, during the war. He was elected to the Senate in 1870.

HIRAM REVELS

EYEWITNESS

"February 3, 1872: The sun shines beautifully today. Our garden has been reploughed. I am so proud of the prospect of a flower yard & the orchard improvement that I feel like one just embracing the threshold of a new life. I find now the study of agriculture most necessary."

MARY VIRGINIA LEWIS,
in a diary excerpt

Davis Bend, Mississippi

In rural Mississippi before the Civil War, Benjamin T. Montgomery was admired by his fellow slaves on the Davis cotton plantation. Montgomery was an inventor, a machinist, and most of all, a born leader. After the war, Montgomery and his fellow African Americans founded a model community on the former plantation of Jefferson Davis that amazed critics and supporters alike.

The black farming community flourished. By 1865 the field force had produced almost two thousand bales of cotton and made a large profit. The African Americans elected their own sheriffs and judges. Benjamin Montgomery, not surprisingly, served as justice of the peace.

Montgomery's wife, Mary Lewis, initiated her own planting operation on 130 acres by employing orphaned children. Her Home Farm gained fame when she produced the "best bale of cotton" at the 1870 St. Louis Fair. Her two daughters, Mary Virginia and Rebecca, practiced piano and stitched needlepoint like other young Southern women, but six days a week they worked in the family store.

Market day in the "Cotton South," 1880.

Mary Virginia's diary describes a life full of talent and promise. This accomplished twenty-three-year-old woman confronted Jefferson Davis in 1872 when he paid a call at Brierfield, his former home. He wanted to get his land back from the Montgomerys, but failed. After Reconstruction ended, however, Davis eventually recovered his estate.

Many members of this first generation of black politicians had more humble origins. Alonzo Ransier worked his way up from shipping clerk to become the first African-American lieutenant governor of South Carolina in 1870. Charles E. Nash, a bricklayer in Louisiana before the war, who lost a leg in combat, served one term in Congress. Josiah T. Walls of Florida, a farmer, was the only black elected to serve from his state.

War hero Robert Smalls was a congressional delegate from South Carolina. He served alongside other former slaves, including Benjamin Turner of Alabama; John R. Lynch of Mississippi; Jeremiah Haralson of Alabama; Robert C. DeLarge of South Carolina; John A. Hyman of North Carolina; and Jefferson F. Long of Georgia.

Blanche K. Bruce was elected to the Mississippi state legislature and then to the U.S. Senate. Not only did Bruce champion his fellow African Americans, but he fought for the rights of Chinese immigrants and Native Americans. Louisiana politician P.B.S. Pinchback held more political offices than any other Reconstruction figure.

This incomplete listing of African-American politicians does not even begin to capture the enormous significance of black legislators as role models. Hundreds of African Americans from the North migrated south to participate in this historic change. They served proudly during this brief but momentous era of black officeholding.

This Democratic party cartoon suggests that federal soldiers forced free black voters to cast ballots only for the Republicans. Opponents of black suffrage complained that former slaves were puppets at the mercy of unscrupulous carpetbaggers. (Note the carpetbag in the right foreground.)

A poster celebrating the rapid rise of African-American politicians during the era following the Civil War.

THE END OF RECONSTRUCTION, 1877

By 1876 many white Southerners had joined Democrats in the North to oppose Republican rule. The Republicans had been in charge of Washington for nearly sixteen years, and many felt that they had abused their power. When Republican presidential nominee Rutherford B. Hayes declared a victory over Democrat Samuel Tilden in November 1876, election results in several Southern states were disputed. Republicans and Democrats had to find a solution that would not divide the country again.

After months of bickering, a compromise was reached: Even though he had been defeated in the popular vote, Hayes was declared winner of the election. In return, the government withdrew federal soldiers from all Southern states. Shortly thereafter, Southern states began to pass legislation to segregate—or separate on the basis of race—public facilities such as parks, schools, restaurants, and even public water fountains. These rules, known as "Jim Crow laws" (after a clownlike black character in vaudeville), reduced African Americans in the South to second-class citizens. This situation was a crushing blow, especially for those blacks who had fought during the Civil War and risked their lives to secure a better life for their children. For former Confederates who had fought so long and hard to overthrow the Yankees, the repeal of the laws and the withdrawal of federal troops was clearly a victory.

Almost from the moment of surrender, participants and historians, politicians and schoolchildren, began to debate about the meaning of the Civil War—or really, its many meanings. Divided over who was to blame for the tragic death toll, Americans nevertheless united in mourning for the forfeit of a generation whose talents and energies were forever lost.

Civil War statues decorate town squares from rural Mississippi to New York City. These hundreds, even thousands, of memorials remind us of the bravery of those who died for their beliefs, nearly six hundred thousand soldiers. In today's terms, equivalent losses would total more than five million men. Many of the battlefields where they fought have been preserved as parks. When soldiers came home from the Civil War, sectional and racial debates continued. Americans wanted to know: Would we still fulfill our destiny, and what might that destiny be? Would we grant full and equal status to all our citizens? Would Americans accept the Confederate cultural heritage on equal footing? Would we incorporate the struggles of African Americans into our Civil War legacy?

After the Confederate surrender, white Southerners resisted the imposition of federal rule, but former slaves welcomed the intervention of the national government. The economy of the South had been destroyed by war. Cotton never again reached its prewar status, the plantation system was crippled in the wake of emancipation, and white politicians saw their power stifled as well.

During the centennial of the Civil War, (its one-hundredth anniversary) in the 1960s, the United States was still divided on the question of rights for

Nearly one hundred years after the end of slavery, African Americans staged a "sit-in" at a lunch counter reserved "For Whites Only." These boycotts and other protests of the 1960s demanded civil rights for all citizens, regardless of race.

A March on Washington on August 28, 1963, where the Reverend Martin Luther King, Jr., gave his "I Have a Dream" speech, brought nearly a quarter million protesters to the nation's capital demanding "Jobs and Freedom!"

Veterans of Pickett's Charge gathered on the fiftieth anniversary of the Battle of Gettysburg in 1913.

African Americans versus states' rights in the South. Since the postwar era, blacks had been involved in protest movements—fighting for the vote, battling to end lynching, and challenging segregation. From 1876 on, the South witnessed several major migrations of African Americans moving northward in search of better conditions and racial tolerance. Unfortunately, many black migrants found that racism plagued the North, as well as the South.

During the 1960s, the government struggled to fulfill the promises of the Thirteenth, Fourteenth, and Fifteenth amendments. All African Americans, especially those in the South, demanded that the federal government intervene to protect civil and human rights. Martin Luther King, Jr., a southern-born, northern-educated black minister, inspired a younger generation of African Americans to protest unfair treatment. A new generation of activists led boycotts and "sit-ins," where blacks sought accommodation at "white only" facilities; freedom rides, where blacks and whites sat together rather than apart on interstate buses in southern states; and other campaigns for civil rights.

During this era Americans witnessed some of the most important legislation of the twentieth century, including the Civil Rights Act of 1964 and the Voting Rights Act of 1965. These reforms were pushed through Congress by another President Johnson—Lyndon Baines Johnson—who was only the second southerner to occupy the White House since the Civil War.

Americans maintain strong and in some cases opposing viewpoints about the causes of the Civil War, the significance of its outcome, and the content of its legacy today. Regardless of debates, America's democratic heritage was strengthened by the long and bloody struggle. States' rights were certainly diminished, and the mighty South clearly fell on hard times, but the nation reunified and emerged whole.

Perhaps the costs of war cannot be measured effectively on a balance sheet. Instead, we must consider what we can learn from our Civil War, what we can take away from this cataclysmic event. In a world where civil wars are common and democracies are struggling to emerge and survive, the American Civil War remains a beacon of hope—as well as one of history's most vivid examples of the tragedy of war.

EYEWITNESS

"*America has no North, no South, no East, no West. The sun rises over the hills and sets over the mountains. The compass just points up and down, and we can laugh now at the absurd notion of there being a North and a South ... we are one and undivided.*"

SAM WATKINS,
Civil War veteran

INDEX

Glorieta Pass, battle of, 40
Grant, Gen. Ulysses S., 39–41, 51, 57, 67,
     72, 73, 75–77, 79–81, 99, 101, 104
Greenhow, Rose, 91
guerrillas (outlaw soldiers), 17, 86

Hamlin, Hannibal, 89
Hammond, James Henry, 17
Hampton Roads, battle of, 41
Hannibal Guards, 34
Harpers Ferry (VA), 18–19, 25
Harper's Weekly, 24, 83, 88, 104
Hayes, Rutherford B., 107
Hill, Gen. A. P., 64
home front, 33, 48–49
Homer, Winslow, 80, 83
Hood, Gen. John Bell, 84, 90
Hooker, Gen. Joseph, 62–63, 72
Howard, Gen. Oliver O., 96
Hunchback, U.S.S., 26
Hunter, Gen. David, 59, 84–85

Illustrated London News, The, 83
infantry, 28
Irish immigrants, 55, 82
"ironclads," 41

Jackson, Andrew, 11
Jackson, Gen. Thomas J. ("Stonewall"),
     32, 39, 44–45, 47, 62–63
Jefferson, Thomas, 9
Jim Crow laws, 107
Johnson, Andrew, 88, 89, 95, 101, 102, 104
Johnson, Lyndon Baines, 109
Johnston, Gen. Albert Sidney, 41
Johnston, Gen. Joseph E., 32, 44, 84, 90,
     99

Kansas-Nebraska Act of 1854, 16–17
Kennesaw Mountain (GA), battle of, 84
King, Martin Luther, Jr., 109
Ku Klux Klan, 104

Lawrence (KS), 17, 86
Lee, Gen. Robert E., 18, 32, 39, 44, 47,
     50–51, 57, 62–66, 76–77, 79, 95, 98, 99
Liberator, The (newspaper), 12
Lincoln, Abraham
     assassination of, 95, 100–101
     on blacks in the military, 34
     as commander-in-chief, 33, 37, 39, 51,
          55, 66, 72, 98
     Gettysburg Address by, 70, 71
     as president, 19, 23, 28, 86, 88–89, 97
     and slavery issues, 51, 55, 57, 58, 96
Lincoln, Mary Todd, 49, 70
Lincoln-Douglas debates, 19

Longstreet, Gen. James, 47, 48, 66, 70,
     76–77
Louisiana Purchase, 9, 16
Lowe, Thaddeus, 53
Lyon, Gen. Nathaniel, 33

Madison, James, 9
Malvern Hill (VA), battle at, 46
Manassas Junction (VA)
     first battle of, 21, 32–33
     second battle of, 47
March on Washington (1963), 108
March to the Sea, Sherman's, 92–93
Martin, Rev. Sella, 35
Mason, Charles, 7
Mason-Dixon line, 7, 9
McClellan, Gen. George, 33, 39, 44, 46, 47,
     50–51, 88–89
McDowell, Gen. Irvin, 32, 33
McLean, Wilmer, 98, 99
Meade, Gen. George, 63, 64, 65
Meagher, Thomas Francis, 55
Mechanicsville (VA), battle at, 46
medical care
     amputation, 30, 61
     at Andersonville Prison, 103
     for Confederate wounded, 60, 61
     by conscientious objectors, 51
     sanitary conditions, 31
     for Union wounded, 31, 61
Merrimack, U.S.S., 41
Mexico, 11, 14, 105
military service
     by blacks, 34–35, 55, 57, 58–59,
          68–69
     camp life, 29, 43
     by children, 43, 70
     conscientious objection to, 51, 82
     draft riots against, 68
     exemptions from, 68
     by Irish immigrants, 55, 82
     by Native Americans, 73, 82
     in non-combat roles, 28–29, 51
     by substitutes, 68
     by women, 47, 59
military tactics, 28, 75, 79, 84, 85, 93
military terms, defined, 28 (box)
Milledgeville (GA) arsenal, 92
Mississippi River, 27, 42, 51, 56–57, 67
Missouri Compromise, 9, 16
Monitor, U.S.S., 41
Mosby, Col. John Singleton, 85
Mudd, Dr. Samuel, 101
Murfreesboro (TN), battle of, 54

Nashville, battle of, 90
Natchez (MS), Union capture of, 42

Native Americans, 73, 82, 90
New Orleans, 8, 11, 42
New York City, 8, 68
newspapers, 82–83
North Star, The (newspaper), 12
nullification, doctrine of, 10
nursing profession, 31, 61

Oak Grove (VA), battle at, 46
Ohio River, 9
O'Sullivan, Timothy, 53

Pacifism, 51, 82
Parker, Col. Ely, 73
Parker, William, 15
Petersburg (VA), 79, 80–81
photography, 45, 52–53
Pickett, Gen. George, 66
"Pikes Peakers," 40
Pinkerton, Allan, 91
plantation economy, 8–9, 17, 108
"plug-uglies," 25
Polk, James K., 11
pontoon bridges, 54
Pope, Gen. John, 46, 47
Port Gibson, 67
Port Hudson (LA), 42, 69
Port Royal (SC), 36–37
Porter, Adm. David, 76, 98
Powell (Payne), Lewis, 101
Price, Gen. Sterling, 86, 105
prison conditions, 73, 92, 103

Quakers (Society of Friends), 12, 51
Quantrill, William Clarke, 86

Racial equality, 34, 58, 105
racism, persistence of, 109
Radical Republicans, 102, 104
railroad bridges, 52, 53
railroads, 30, 32, 53, 92
Rebel yell, 32
Reconstruction, 95, 102, 104, 105, 107
Red Cross, American, 31
Red River, 76
Republican party, 17, 19, 28, 88
Richmond (VA)
     bread riots in, 60
     Confederate capital moved to, 25
     Union campaigns against, 38–39, 44,
          46, 54, 77, 78, 80
     Union capture of, 94–95, 98
Ripley, Elizabeth, 42
Robertson, John, 60
Rogers, Dr. S. W., 101
Rosencrans, Gen. William S., 54, 70
Ross, John (Cherokee chief), 82

PHOTO CREDITS

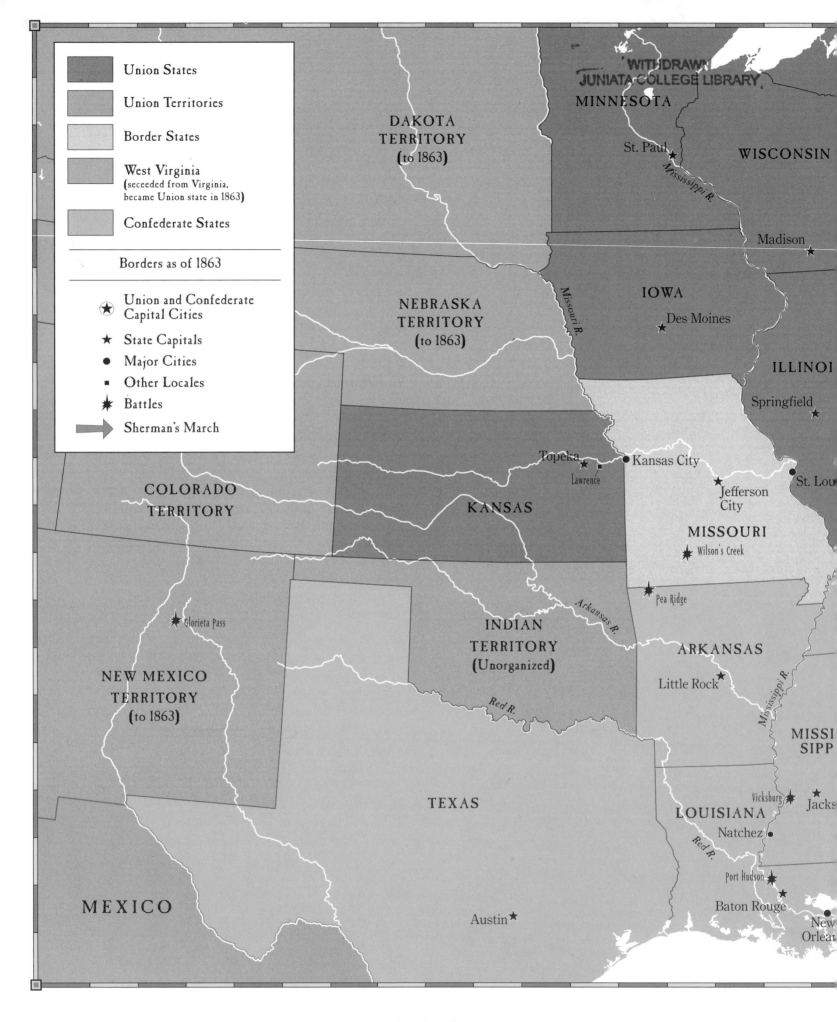

Union States

Union Territories

Border States

West Virginia
(seceded from Virginia, became Union state in 1863)

Confederate States

Borders as of 1863

⊛ Union and Confederate Capital Cities

★ State Capitals

● Major Cities

■ Other Locales

✳ Battles

➡ Sherman's March

MINNESOTA

WISCONSIN

St. Paul ★

Mississippi R.

Madison ★

DAKOTA TERRITORY (to 1863)

IOWA

Des Moines ★

Missouri R.

ILLINOI

NEBRASKA TERRITORY (to 1863)

Springfield ★

COLORADO TERRITORY

Topeka ★ ■ ● Kansas City
Lawrence

Jefferson City ★

● St. Lou

KANSAS

MISSOURI

✳ Wilson's Creek

Glorieta Pass ✳

Arkansas R.

✳ Pea Ridge

INDIAN TERRITORY (Unorganized)

ARKANSAS

NEW MEXICO TERRITORY (to 1863)

Little Rock ★

Red R.

Mississippi R.

MISSI SIPPI

TEXAS

Vicksburg ✳ Jacks ★

LOUISIANA

Natchez ●

Red R.

MEXICO

Port Hudson ✳

Baton Rouge ★

Austin ★

New Orlean